AMONG
ENEMIES

AMONG ENEMIES

Counter-Espionage
FOR THE
BUSINESS TRAVELER

Luke Bencie

MOUNTAIN LAKE PRESS

MOUNTAIN LAKE PARK, MARYLAND

Among Enemies
Counter-Espionage for the Business Traveler

© 2013 Luke Bencie
All Rights Reserved

Published in the United States of America

Mountain Lake Press

mountainlakepress.com

ISBN: 978-0-9885919-1-2

LIBRARY OF CONGRESS
CONTROL NUMBER 2012953730

Design by Michael Hentges

*To my parents, for always reminding me
that it is not how you start but how you finish;
to my beautiful wife, for her unconditional love and patience
while I traveled the world;
and to the men and women of the intelligence community,
who serve in the shadows to keep this country safe*

Counter-Espionage

"The aspect of counterintelligence designed to detect,
destroy, neutralize, exploit, or prevent espionage activities
through identification, penetration, manipulation, deception,
and repression of individuals, groups, or organizations
conducting or suspected of conducting espionage activities."

– U.S. Department of Defense
Dictionary of Military and Associated Terms

Contents

Foreword

In this age of international terrorism, overseas business travelers constantly have to worry about the possibility of becoming victims. They avoid certain countries, stick to familiar and relatively safe venues and carriers, and even rely on hired security people to protect them. But there is another activity that increasingly threatens overseas travelers. It may not be as potentially lethal as terrorism, but it is just as real, quite costly and much more likely to cause them harm.

It is economic espionage.

I spent over 30 years with the Federal Bureau of Investigation. There, I headed up major criminal investigations, I oversaw the FBI's activities overseas and I recommended staff levels and procedures necessary to protect our citizens abroad. So, I fully comprehend the risks involved. These predators who conduct economic espionage – both in the service of foreign governments and as independent operators – also kidnap for ransom, steal trade secrets and commit a host of other crimes, all aimed at business travelers and their companies. This is happening at a time when American firms are looking to expand their role in the global economy, particularly in developing countries.

My familiarity with this situation has intensified since I left the bureau. I have served as corporate security director for a Fortune 500 financial concern with a large international presence, and I have taught homeland security and international terrorism courses as an adjunct professor. In these roles, as well as in my private life, people who travel for business often ask me about their safety overseas; likewise those who travel for pleasure. So do parents of students abroad. They all consistently seek advice on how to avoid becoming victims – or, worse, casualties.

These concerns are well founded, but there are ways to reduce the dangers. *Among Enemies: Counter-Espionage for the Business Traveler* serves as the perfect resource for beginning this process – for helping to prevent a personal or business catastrophe.

Luke Bencie, the author, has worked in the U.S. intelligence community as well as in the world of private defense contracting. He has developed a reputation for consummate professionalism, for being keenly knowledgeable in his area of expertise, and for possessing a genuine concern for Americans traveling abroad.

I worked with Luke after I left the government. Over the years, I have come to know him personally, and I have seen how his extensive international experience allows him to approach the subject of economic espionage from a skilled and sensible point of view. I regard him as the ideal person to write this book.

Luke explains why people conduct economic espionage, who the people are that commit these crimes, and – most important – how they gain proprietary information. He arms travelers with simple safeguards to protect both themselves personally and the secrets of the businesses they represent.

For example, today's international travelers routinely carry an array of electronic devices – from laptop computers and iPads or other digital tablets, and their associated data-storage devices, to smartphones and HD-video cameras. Luke dedicates a chapter to protecting these devices from cyber intrusions and remote data theft. His real-life examples vividly demonstrate how commonplace these crimes can be. They could easily make you stop and say, "Hey – that could have been me!" He also explains why it is just as important to be on guard in the United Kingdom or France as it is in a competitive or outright unfriendly country, such as China or Iran.

For these reasons, you should consider *Among Enemies* a must-read if you travel overseas, whether on business or even to gain an understanding of the hidden threats you could face.

When Luke described his idea of writing a practical book for business travelers that was easy to read but would give solid lessons in counter-espionage, I was surprised such a book had not been written before – but I immediately agreed it was a fabulous idea. Knowing Luke's background, it struck me that with his qualifications and attention to detail he could educate travelers better than anyone about what could happen to them or their company if they let their guard down.

Recently, I heard a government official speaking on public radio about the rise in economic espionage and related prosecutions in the last few years. The official said cases had more than doubled in 2012, apparently because many countries and companies are using espionage to save time and money on research and development.

That revelation might come as a shock to people who do not understand what economic espionage is or think they could never be targeted by it. They also might underestimate the value of what they know – and who knows what they know. But individuals dealing in economic espionage make it a point to learn who each traveler is and what information he or she might possess. They also attempt to learn what devices these individuals are carrying and how to gain access to them. I know this, and so does Luke Bencie. He has dealt with espionage firsthand, and he uses his valuable experiences as examples throughout the book.

Whether you are heading overseas for the first time or travel on a regular basis, you owe it to yourself to read *Among Enemies*. Fortunately, it is an easy read. It offers simple rules, it makes sense and it will educate you about how economic espionage works and how to counteract it. It will help you lower your risk of becoming a victim.

A friend of mine recently traveled to a European capital with his wife to celebrate their wedding anniversary. They checked into a five-star hotel and were offered a complimentary massage. They set up a time for the session the day they arrived. During that session, thieves entered their room and took their jewelry, credit cards and passports – even items locked in the room safe. What should have been a memorable vacation turned into a nightmare.

This type of incident can happen to anyone traveling abroad, and *Among Enemies: Counter-Espionage for the Business Traveler* can provide you with the knowledge to prevent it and protect yourself, your business and your intellectual property.

I strongly recommend it.

William J. Esposito
Former Deputy Director
Federal Bureau of Investigation

Introduction

"Counter-espionage is inherently a protective and defensive operation."
– Allen Dulles, legendary CIA director

Picture this: John is a mid-level manager at a Fortune 1000 company in a major American city. He could be in software, manufacturing or financial services; perhaps pharmaceuticals, communications, energy or construction. He's just concluded a new business agreement in principle with a company in China, and tonight he's flying to Shanghai to meet his new partners and sign contracts. He can't help thinking about what this deal portends for him and his company.

John settles into his business-class seat for the long flight on this, his first trip to Asia. As he taps out some last-minute messages on his smartphone, a beautiful Asian woman takes the seat next to him, smiling and flashing her almond eyes. Like her silky black hair, her legs are long and sensual. She smells incredible. She and John exchange pleasantries. He discovers she is Chinese, heading home to visit her parents. She asks why he's flying to Shanghai, and he proudly describes his company's ties to its new business partner there. She tells him she works as an English-Chinese translator and offers to teach him some important phrases and gestures to help him in his meetings.

John has more work to do on the plane, so he politely disengages himself, opens his laptop, and plans to fill the time and distance productively. As night falls, however, the Chinese woman becomes more talkative and friendly – and distracting. She begins flirting, and the two of them share laughs over champagne, keeping the flight attendant busy refilling their glasses.

John finds the business-class dinner especially tasty: filet mignon with truffle butter and a side of creamed spinach. His devotion to career has kept him away from the dating scene for a number of years, so he's pleasantly surprised at how comfortable he feels with this beautiful woman and how well she is responding to his banter. Eventually, she falls asleep on his shoulder, and soon he's asleep as well. When he awakens, she has already brushed her hair and put on fresh makeup, and the flight attendant is asking what the couple wants for breakfast.

This flight is passing too quickly! John thinks to himself.

After landing, John and the woman clear customs and immigration together. As they walk outside, she asks the name of his hotel. When he tells her, she exclaims that she is staying there as well and offers to hail a taxi for them both. She waves several away then selects one. John follows her in; she smiles at him, and he smiles back. By this time, he's feeling a strong attraction. He invites her to dinner, and she accepts. She suggests that he ask the taxi driver to remain on call during his stay, that it's customary to do so. It seems like a good idea, and she makes the arrangements with him before bidding John adieu for the afternoon, presenting him with her business card and wishing him good luck.

John's first meeting passes cordially, although his Chinese colleagues appear, as he had expected, inscrutable. Their tone is friendly and the conversation optimistic, but they don't want to commit to a contract just yet. John is taken aback by this and presses for another meeting the next morning. They agree and promise to reconsider their position. In the taxi, John calls his CEO stateside on his smartphone and tells him he finds this turn of events troubling. Perhaps it's just jet lag, the CEO responds, encouragingly.

That night, John enjoys a delightful time with his lovely new Chinese friend. They share drinks and dine, and afterward they visit a karaoke bar. There, they order more drinks, and as they sing some corny duets, John becomes less and less inhibited. She subtly shifts the topic of conversation to his business plans and goals.

Back at the hotel, John escorts the woman to her room and, in a stroke of boldness, asks to join her. She smiles sweetly, tells him she's flattered but kisses his cheek and says goodnight. Back in his own room, he realizes he probably has had too much to drink. He stumbles into bed, falling asleep while savoring the memories of the evening – but failing to notice his computer and smartphone have shifted position on the desk.

The following morning, John receives a call on the hotel phone. He learns that the meeting must be postponed; one of the principals is out of the office on urgent business. They expect him back later in the day and will reschedule the meeting as soon as possible. Meanwhile, they ask for a little more information, which John willingly provides.

That afternoon, John receives another call. They apologize again but insist that the meeting must wait until the following day – so many people to bring together, so many details to go over. Frustrated, John goes for a long walk and, upon his return, he phones his Chinese ladyfriend to see if she would like to go out again that evening. The front desk informs him that she has checked out. He goes through his pockets but cannot find her card.

The next morning, John's taxi takes him to the meeting. Upon arrival, his erstwhile Chinese colleagues tell him they have decided to table the partnership for the time being. He feebly protests but is told the decision cannot be helped – again, so much to consider, to plan for, a thousand apologies, but this is how it must be. John becomes upset and reminds them he has worked with them for nearly a year to reach this point. Now, suddenly, there is a problem? Perhaps they don't realize his firm could have chosen another Chinese partner? They show sympathy and assure John they will understand if his company decides to take its business elsewhere.

John returns home angry and dejected, trying to understand what had happened.

Does this story sound implausible, as though it came out of a grade B melodrama? Or, does it sound all too familiar? Has it happened to a colleague – has something similar even happened to you?

Maybe you have figured out the plot: Our fictional business traveler became a mark, the victim of economic espionage, intended – in this case successfully – to steal valuable business intelligence.

My tale might be fictional, but it isn't fiction. Such scenarios are happening every day around the globe. Here's how this one played out.

The attractive woman on the plane was working for the Chinese company. Her assignment: Obtain as much information as possible about the presumed partnership. Her employers wanted to see if they could cut the American company out of the deal. While the mark slept on the plane, she inserted a flash drive into his computer's USB port and copied everything from his hard disk. She also installed a keystroke-logging program that captured and transmitted everything he typed from then on – including his passwords.

Like the woman, the taxi driver was an espionage operative. She had hired him on behalf of her company. His job was to record phone conversations, track where the mark went during his visit and report any other information the company might use to competitive advantage – all of which the woman relayed to her employer.

The taxi driver also freelanced as a business intelligence collector. Aware that the traveler was a mark, the driver offered his information – that some kind of big business deal was going down – to the hotel concierge, who paid him for the tip and sold it to a Chinese information peddler, known as a private collector. While the American and his new Chinese friend went out for the evening, the concierge let the private collector into the mark's room, where he downloaded information from the laptop and smartphone, scanned all paper documents in the mark's briefcase, and bugged the room telephone.

The private collector studied the stolen information and contacted a competitor he thought would be interested in the business intelligence. Meanwhile, the Chinese company, using its own corporate intelligence agents, learned that details of the potential partnership had been compromised, and the American's business intelligence was sold to a competitor.

The company had delayed the second meeting to assess the nature and scope of the leak and how it might hurt them. They determined that if they moved forward with the partnership they would not enjoy a competitive advantage. To them, the American businessman had lost face for allowing his information to be stolen and compromised, rendering his company an undesirable partner. They killed the deal with typical Asian courtesy then immediately began reconfiguring their original plan to outwit both the American partner and their Chinese competitors and beat them all to market. Everything I have described here is based on fact and real-life experience. Any and all of these events – or worse – could happen to you. The cleverness and sophistication portrayed in this example suggest that many American business travelers remain naïve about such threats.

At this point, you might be thinking, "I travel to Europe once a month to make a sales call on a customer I've been servicing for years. Why would anybody want to follow me or hack into my computer? I'm not a spy; I'm an account executive!"

"No," you're insisting, "this could *never* happen to me."

You may prefer to stick with this conceit, but believe me: Anytime you travel abroad, you're likely to become the target of the intelligence services of foreign governments and other business intelligence-gathering entities. You might not be a spy, but you're going to be treated like one – meaning you and your belongings will be monitored, and your proprietary information could be stolen without your knowledge.

Therefore, *never* be so naïve as to think your presence or the information you carry is of no interest to others.

To paraphrase a movie line: Be concerned; be very concerned. But you need not be afraid. This book will help you learn how to translate your concern into action by thinking and acting like a counterintelligence officer.

How do I know? Because I've worked in the intelligence community for many years, and later I worked as one of those international defense contractors who are so frequently targeted by unfriendly foreign governments.

In that capacity, I've been mugged, drugged, arrested, detained, bombed, robbed, shot at, videotaped, compromised, elicited, blackmailed, lied to, intimidated, jailed, questioned and refused access.

In other words, I've been there.

Just like my fictional businessman, I've been followed by a surveillance team. I've also had audio and video devices planted in my hotel room and vehicle. I've been approached by strangers trying to elicit confidential information from me in casual settings. I've been offered a briefcase full of cash for my secrets. I've been approached by beautiful women whose intentions were to put me in compromising situations for purposes of blackmail. And I've been detained by foreign authorities to prevent me from, in their words, "stirring up trouble."

You should also know – and never forget – that espionage and terrorism are two sides of the same coin. Following September 11, 2001, I participated in counterterrorism operations overseas in Iraq, Afghanistan and other countries in the Middle East. I've trained thousands of domestic and international police, military and intelligence service personnel in border security, counterintelligence, threat/surveillance detection, counterfeiting and piracy, and recognizing and discouraging terrorist movement across borders.

So, please, take my word for it. This is a serious matter that puts not only you at risk but also our global economic future. With this book, I will give you the tools necessary to defend yourself against economic espionage.

Luke Bencie, *Managing Director*
Security Management International, LLC

January 2013
Falls Church, Virginia

1. Everything Has Changed

"The most valuable commodity I know of is information."
– Gordon Gekko, in the movie *Wall Street*

The Risks of Business Travel in the 21st-Century Global Economy

Have you ever wondered why you have to fill out an information card when you check in at a hotel, or why your passport is photocopied or scanned? You might think you're providing identity verification, but think again. In many countries, a representative from the "Ministry of the Interior," or a bureaucratic equivalent, will drop by the desk each night to collect the information so the local intelligence service can track who is in the country. That service will attempt to identify which individuals should be considered persons of interest.

In my work, I've traveled to more than 120 of the world's 194 countries and stayed in thousands of places, so I'm familiar with the drill. I once checked into a popular hotel in North Africa. There, I had to forfeit my passport for two days while it was copied, my visa stamps studied and my travel patterns analyzed. The bellboy trotted off with my bags into a so-called service elevator. Before he delivered them to my room, half an hour later, someone obviously had opened and searched them.

That little detour had set off my mental alarm bells, so I scanned my room with a surveillance-detection device I had purchased at a spy shop in London. The device looks like an automobile's remote-entry keychain fob. It detected a microphone disguised as a button on the sofa. I didn't remove or disrupt it, but thereafter I never spoke a word in the room.

Outside the hotel, I spotted an intelligence officer following my every move, but I never let on that I knew I was being surveilled. The agent knew I knew but never let on that he knew I knew. In other words, we both played the game and did our jobs.

"Espionage? Are you kidding? That's the stuff of James Bond movies!"

"Steal trade secrets from me? Ha! I don't have anything that would interest a spy."

"Hey, come on, the Cold War is long over."

"Spies in hotels? Don't you think you're acting paranoid?"

These comments were made recently by American businesspeople waiting for their flights at JFK International Airport. They had been asked what they knew about the theft of billions of dollars worth of information annually from business travelers just like themselves. Although a few expressed interest, none seemed fully aware of the threat – to them personally or to the business intelligence they carried.

insider tale

Economic Espionage: The FBI's Second-Highest Priority

If there were no risk or danger, would the FBI be actively fighting economic espionage? C. Frank Figliuzzi, assistant director of the bureau's Counterintelligence Division, testified June 28, 2012, before the U.S. House of Representatives Subcommittee on Counterterrorism and Intelligence. The hearing's subject was "Economic Espionage: A Foreign Intelligence Threat to American Jobs and Homeland Security."

Figliuzzi made the following points:

—"In the FBI's pending caseload for the current fiscal year, economic-espionage losses to the American economy total more than $13 billion. The health of America's companies is vital to our economy, and our economy is a matter of national security."

—"Each year, foreign intelligence services and their collectors become more creative and more sophisticated in their methods to undermine American business and erode the one thing that most provides American business its leading edge: our ability to innovate."

—The threat is growing more pervasive due in part to "increasing exposure to foreign intelligence services presented by the reality of global business, joint ventures, and the growing international footprint of American firms."[1]

There is great risk in losing or compromising important information or intelligence. Essentially, it has always been so. Over the centuries, couriers for Alexander the Great, Hannibal, Genghis Kahn and other warriors routinely carried documents with news, orders or plans for ongoing wars and battles. If they were spotted, they were usually tracked, attacked and killed, their valuable intelligence taken and used by the enemy.

Think of yourself, the business traveler, as one of those couriers when you carry your company's valuable information. The enemy is an espionage operative waiting for the right moment to pounce. Whether physical, electronic or cybernetic, their thefts are usually so sophisticated you don't even know they are occurring, and this poses the greatest threat of all.

Ever heard of Boeing? How about Archer Daniels Midland? Or Dow Chemical, DuPont, American Superconductor, Ford, Apple, Lockheed Martin or Google? They represent only the tip of the economic-espionage iceberg, because all have been targeted successfully by operatives. Losses of this type to U.S. corporations doing business internationally are difficult to track, because they're not reported formally – and most companies don't want to admit them – but by my own estimates they run as high as $300 billion a year.

Indeed, sometimes companies don't even know their proprietary information has been stolen, until it appears in another company's offering – or as a competitor's product. In the 21st century, business information can be more valuable than government or military information.

Bottom line: As one of the 35,000 U.S. business travelers flying daily to domestic and international meetings, you and your valuable information are very much at risk.

Two Primary Rules for Business Travelers

You want to be aware of the risks to yourself and your information when you're traveling. You want to understand how you can secure and protect your information from misappropriation or theft.

Here's what you must do:

Rule 1. Assume at all times you are being surveilled by someone who wants your information.

If you do this, and do it consistently, you're taking the first and most important step in protecting your information from those who would take it from you.

Rule 2. Learn to think and act like a counterintelligence officer.

What exactly is a counterintelligence officer? There are many definitions, depending on whom you ask – there are dozens of definitions in the United States alone, for example. But for the purposes of this book, we will use language from The National Security Act of 1947, the legislation that gave the CIA its power.

According to that legislation, a counterintelligence officer performs counterintelligence, defined as "information gathered and activities conducted to protect against espionage, other intelligence activities, sabotage or assassinations conducted for or on behalf of foreign governments or elements thereof, foreign organizations or foreign persons or international terrorist activities."

Let me further clarify: counter-espionage is actually a subset of counterintelligence. Counterintelligence encompasses many facets of the intelligence world, but counter-espionage focuses on one theme: repelling the penetration – or getting inside – by a foreign organization. Because no one is formally called a counter-espionage officer, for this book's purposes just assume you're receiving training as a counterintelligence officer.

What Are We Trying to Protect?

We'll use the terms business intelligence and intellectual property, shortened to the acronym BI/IP, to characterize your valuable information.

Business intelligence is proprietary information used for strategic decision-making and analyzing business performance. Examples include business plans, meeting memos, P&L spreadsheets, product R&D and sales figures.

Intellectual property is the tangible expression and manifestation of an original idea that can be identified as belonging to its owner and, in many cases, protected by patent, copyright or ownership laws. Examples include software programs, business processes and methodologies, patents, copyrights and trademarks, or formal diagnostic or analytical tools.

Taken together, whenever intelligence or information can be gathered, analyzed and managed in such a way that it informs others of your plans, decisions or operations, it is considered competitive intelligence.

Your most important task as a business traveler is to protect these assets, which may take one or more of the following forms. Which do you carry?

- ☐ Acquisitions, mergers and negotiation strategies
- ☐ Agreements, correspondence and memoranda
- ☐ Business strategies, goals, plans and objectives
- ☐ Command and control procedures
- ☐ Communications frequencies (via electronic devices)
- ☐ Computer network designs and protocols
- ☐ Conference and meeting schedules
- ☐ Corporate financial and investment data
- ☐ Customer and business-alliance data
- ☐ Internal or industrial language
- ☐ IP access control lists (ACLs)
- ☐ Logistics and delivery or work schedules
- ☐ Marketing and sales strategies and information
- ☐ Passwords and logins
- ☐ Personnel background information and phone directories
- ☐ Project names, reports and spreadsheet data
- ☐ Proposals, bids and pricing strategies
- ☐ Proprietary formulas and processes
- ☐ Reports
- ☐ R&D prototypes
- ☐ Security and emergency operations records and procedures
- ☐ Standard operating procedures
- ☐ Stock numbers, inventory reports and manufacturing data
- ☐ Training programs, documentation, requirements and capabilities
- ☐ Technical systems, components and plans
- ☐ Vendor information

Remember **Rule 1:** Assume at all times you are being surveilled.

Assume as well you are being surveilled by someone who wants your BI/IP. Think I'm being overly paranoid here? If you consider that on a typical day in London it is estimated that a person can be captured on video by 300 CCTV cameras, then paranoia on an Orwellian scale should begin to resonate.

Economic Espionage and Competitive Advantage

We live and work in a fiercely competitive business environment. Companies, foreign and domestic, want your BI/IP to gain a competitive advantage in the marketplace. Even if it weren't illegal to steal BI/IP, it is surely unethical.

Leo Labaj, a retired CIA Technical Operations Officer and my colleague at Security Management International, has worked in vulnerability assessment and counterterrorism for over 40 years. "Businesses know economic espionage is happening," he says. "All they really want is to preserve a six-month competitive edge; that's about all they can expect. [Counter-espionage] is about trying to sustain that economic advantage for as long as possible."

Economic-espionage operatives who would relieve you of your BI/IP fall into three categories: government, corporate and freelancers, also known as private collectors.

Agents of governments will steal your business information to help their countries gain competitive advantage. Their surveillance often begins at customs and immigration points, or generally within an airport, by profiling your clothing, briefcase or other attributes of your appearance. This type of espionage is practiced most frequently by countries where there is a strong cooperative relationship between government and business.

Trained corporate espionage operatives – in some cases former intelligence officers – will target and shadow you from the outset of your trip. They will seize any opportunity to copy or steal your information from unprotected and unattended belongings, mobile devices and computers. They might be working for the company with which you hope to do business. Or, they might be employed by a competitor or are freelancing within the industry. They also hire observers to identify and surveil business travelers. These individuals can range from skycaps, taxi drivers and hotel clerks to casual contacts in restaurants, bars and, often, office buildings.

Private collectors are freelance spies who mark business travelers in airports and other public places to begin tracking and surveilling them. Their techniques commonly include elicitation – which we'll discuss in the next chapter – hacking public Wi-Fi networks or breaking into hotel rooms to gather whatever information they can find. Then they analyze the information to determine who would be interested and offer it to the highest bidder.

Economic espionage is occurring right now in nearly every country, though most actively in Afghanistan, China, France, India, Iran, Iraq, Israel, Japan, Pakistan, Russia, Taiwan, Thailand and the United Kingdom, as well as in the United States. Why? To help businesses and often their nation-state partners obtain competitive advantage and grow their economies. The playing field is global, and the stakes are high. No country wants to become a has-been in the game of economic success. If they must play dirty – by spying, swindling or stealing – they'll do it, because it's part of what everybody else is doing.

insider tale
An Espionage Hotbed
The country calling itself The Middle Kingdom represents the greatest threat to the U.S. economy. Brett M. Decker, a Washington Post editor and co-author (with William C. Triplett II) of *Bowing to Beijing: How Barack Obama Is Hastening America's Decline and Ushering a Century of Chinese Domination*, said in an interview that the Chinese "are willing to do anything – purchase our national debt, steal our intellectual property, spend obscene amounts to buy influence in Washington, engage in extensive espionage in our government and large corporations, and sell sensitive missile and nuclear technology to our mortal enemies – to defeat us." [2]

Need more evidence? Consider that within *hours* of the 2011 raid by U.S. Navy SEALs on Usama bin Laden's compound in Pakistan, Chinese operatives reportedly attempted to acquire technical intelligence about a secret U.S. helicopter that had crashed during the raid.

Preying on Americans' Vulnerabilities

The United States of America is the land of the greatest ideas and innovations. Its citizens are proud that they've led the world for well over a century in developing innovative solutions to all kinds of needs and problems.

Sometimes that pride gets Americans into trouble, however. They love to tell others – even complete strangers – about their work, company, successes; you name it. They freely pass out Web site URLs, email addresses and phone numbers with their business cards.

The result? Without intending to, well-meaning businesspeople often give away the farm. For their competitors, it makes more economic and business sense to capture the best expertise already available than to struggle for years developing the same BI/IP on their own. At a much lower cost, these entities can capture tried-and-true technologies to get products and services to market better, faster and less expensively. The booty includes proprietary proposal estimates, design specifications, emerging technologies and investment strategies.

> **insider tale**
> **Ignorance Isn't Bliss**
> ASIS International, the world's largest organization for security professionals, advises that security has become too important to be handled by defense experts alone.
> "The growing recognition of Enterprise Security Risk Man¬agement as a holistic view of risk – all risks – throughout an or¬ganization is important," ASIS International advises. "This holistic view helps ensure that the threats that might typically not be recognized in an enterprise risk-management program focusing primarily on financial risks (such overlooked risks, for example, might include risks to brand and reputation, physical supply-chain risks, or loss of consumer confidence if your data is stolen or networks attacked) are now more and more fully identified, prioritized and mitigated." [3]
> Greg Starr, Under Secretary for the Department of Safety and Security at the United Nations, agrees that, "Americans are slow to grasp the risk [involved in international travel]." [4]

ASIS International identifies the following industries as most frequently targeted for BI/IP intelligence theft:

— Aerospace and avionics

— Chemicals and composite materials

— Consumer products

— Educational institutions and services

— Electric utilities and natural resources

— Financial products and services

— Healthcare services

— Information technology and telecommunications

— Life sciences, agriculture and biotechnology

— Motor vehicles and components

— Pharmaceuticals and medical devices

— Transportation

If you work in any of these industries, assume you are a high-profile target. That means you could be targeted every time you leave your office building (and often when you're in it as well). How?

— You can be targeted anytime you use the free Wi-Fi network at Starbucks.

— You're targeted when you use your smartphone in a taxi or your laptop on an airplane.

— You're targeted whether you're traveling domestically or internationally.

As an article in The Washington Post stated, "The guidance security experts give travelers to high-risk countries is extensive: Assume any wireless device will be compromised. Change passwords regularly. Back up information. Do not accept thumb (USB flash) drives as gifts. Do not assume you're too insignificant to be targeted."

Once again, remember **Rule 1**: Assume at all times you are being surveilled by someone who wants your BI/IP.

Technology: The Primary Target

Technology has accelerated every aspect of business and commerce, sometimes for good but often not. Any IT expert will tell you the more open a computer system is, which makes it easier to access and use, the greater the risk it can be hacked.

Today's economic warfare focuses on technology. Business travelers routinely carry sensitive and important BI/IP on their electronic devices. In most cases, those devices are extremely vulnerable to economic espionage.

The threats are not exclusively external, however. Moles and enterprise traitors also operate within the walls of business, capturing whatever BI/IP they think they can sell. Hackers, who could be anywhere on the planet, penetrate computer systems to do the same thing.

insider tale
RATting Out Espionage

In 2009, Dmitri Alperovitch, vice-president of threat research at McAfee, discovered Operation Shady RAT, one of the most insidious cyber-espionage operations ever devised. RAT stands for remote access tool, and beginning in 2006 it attacked more than 70 governments and private businesses, non-profits and think tanks in 14 countries.

Before computer-security experts managed to shut it down, Shady RAT had stolen BI/IP from the governments of Canada, India, South Korea, Taiwan, Vietnam and the United States. The subject matter included agriculture, construction, electronics, energy, defense, media and real estate. Hackers gained access initially through a program called a spear-phishing email, which gave access to data by inserting malware.

Although he has declined to speculate on the source, Alperovitch believes this was a state-sponsored attack.

"I divide the entire set of Fortune Global 2000 firms into two categories: those that know they've been compromised and those that don't yet know," he says, regarding BI/IP. [5]

Taking Matters into Your Own Hands

As an old Yankee saying goes, "If you want something done right, do it yourself."

Without disparaging your company's interest in and efforts to protect its BI/IP, it still falls on your shoulders to take all necessary precautions when you're traveling.

How to do this? You must become your own security staff.

As **Rule 2** points out, learn to think and act like a counterintelligence officer.

An intelligence officer is charged with obtaining and analyzing intelligence for an organization. A counterintelligence officer attempts to detect and assess intelligence threats and deter them.

You might identify the operatives who are attempting to obtain your BI/IP, but your job is not *necessarily* to expose or report them. To do so could create a personal risk in a number of ways. The main objective is defensive, not offensive: think soccer goalie.

Your job is to protect your company's valuable BI/IP without jeopardizing your personal safety. In the chapters that follow, you'll learn how to do this. You will gain a heightened awareness of the treasons and stratagems, to paraphrase Shakespeare's *Merchant of Venice,* being directed at you and your BI/IP, and you will develop the ability to deflect or disable attempts at economic espionage without calling undue attention to yourself or your efforts.

insider tale
Have No Doubt – They're Watching
According to Bill Gertz, a Washington Times national security reporter and New York Times bestselling author, nearly 140 nations and some 35 known and suspected terrorist groups have targeted the United States for espionage.

insider tale
Have No Doubt – They're Active
"The truth I saw was brutal and intense: Electronic thieves are stripping us blind… Technologies that cost millions or billions to develop are being bled out of corporate laboratories via the Internet; or they're slipping out after hours on thumb drives, walking onto airplanes bound for foreign ports, and reentering the country as finished products developed by foreign entrepreneurs. In effect, we're buying back our own technology."

-- Joel Brenner, former inspector general
of the National Security Agency and head of
counterintelligence for the Director of National Intelligence,
in his book *America the Vulnerable: Inside the New Threat
Matrix of Digital Espionage, Crime, and Warfare*

CHAPTER 1 FAQ

1. What can a government do to protect national corporate BI/IP from slipping into enemy hands?

The short answer is: plenty.

In the United States, for example, the Economic Espionage Act of 1996 makes theft of commercial trade secrets a crime punishable by 10 years (or more) in prison for an individual and fines of up to $5 million for companies.

The Federal Bureau of Investigation is actively fighting economic espionage. FBI Director Robert S. Mueller III has designated economic counter-espionage as a top priority, second only to counterterrorism.

The FBI offers the following suggestions for protecting your business from espionage. You would be wise to review them. Read and respond to each question below to determine if you and your company understand what is at stake and if you're taking the right general approach:

☐ Do you recognize there are insider and outsider threats to your company?

☐ Have you identified and evaluated your trade secrets?

☐ Have you implemented a proactive plan for safeguarding your trade secrets?

☐ Have you produced secure physical and electronic versions of your trade secrets?

☐ Do you confine BI/IP to a need-to-know basis?

☐ Does your company train employees to protect BI/IP security?

2. If economic espionage has become one of those "everybody's doing it" phenomena – such as the Japanese copying the technology of American pocket transistor radios back in the 1950s – is it really such a big deal?

Paradoxically, as the global economy has expanded, the competitive playing field has grown smaller and smaller, while competitive advantage has become shorter and shorter lived. National economic health depends on the ability to maintain innovation and keep people employed. That means preventing anyone and everyone from stealing innovation and copying it without having performed the necessary – and expensive – R&D. It's a question of economic survival.

3. What's the best way to fight economic espionage on a personal level?

Keep repeating **Rule** 2: Learn to think and act like a counterintelligence officer. As you'll see, it isn't impossible. In fact, it isn't that difficult, it's a useful skill and if you do it right it can even be fun.

Need to know more?
Email us: questions@among-enemies.com

2. Enemies in Our Midst

> "One good spy is worth 10,000 soldiers"
> – Sun Tzu, *The Art of War*

Who's After You and Your Information,
and How They Try to Get It

According to the *Annual Report to Congress on Foreign Economic Collection and Industrial Espionage*, the United States remains the prime target for these activities by virtue of its global technological leadership and innovation. [6]

Foreign collectors frequently target American travelers overseas. Their marks include businesspeople, government employees and contractors. Collection methods include everything from eliciting information during seemingly innocuous conversations – such as with our fictional Asian lady in the Introduction – to downloading information from laptops or other digital storage devices, for example after surreptitiously entering hotel rooms.

Athletic events such as the FIFA World Cup and the Olympic Games have emerged as useful venues for economic espionage. The reason is obvious. Large corporations often sponsor these events and reward their employees and clients with prime seats and lavish skybox parties. Expensive dinners, where alcohol flows freely, commonly accompany these events. So do attractive young women, many of whom, knowingly or unknowingly, work for private collectors or intelligence services. These women – known as honeypots or honeytraps – can lure business travelers into compromising positions ripe for blackmail.

insider tale
What's Good for the Goose...
Just as men can be enticed by honeypots, females are also susceptible to male Romeos, as they're called. In fact, Sharon Scarange, a former CIA secretary who was posted in Ghana, Africa, pleaded

guilty to espionage when she was caught passing classified documents to her boyfriend, who turned out to be a Ghanaian intelligence officer.

Even the famous Venetian womanizer, Giacomo Casanova, practiced espionage centuries ago. Casanova was accused of trying to sell the secret formula of a red dye to a foreign ambassador.

An even greater emerging threat at major sports venues is from cyber attacks. Don't believe it? Consider that there were more than 500,000 attempted attacks *an hour* – or 12 million a day – at the 2008 Beijing Olympics. Though no statistics have yet been published, a U.K. government official said he anticipated an "astonishing" amount of cybercrime for the 2012 Olympics. Thousands of IT specialists monitored the London games' 11,000 computers, but anyone who connected to an Olympic site was potentially vulnerable to a malware intrusion. [7]

Spying has been called the world's second oldest profession, because there are few more valuable commodities than information. Success, whether personal or professional, often results from accumulating information of the highest utility and quality.

insider tale
The Marine Who Became an Enemy

In 1987, Sgt. Clayton Lonetree was the first U.S. Marine ever convicted of espionage. He was stationed as a guard at the U.S. Embassy in Moscow when he was approached by an attractive woman. Posing as a translator and going by the name Violetta Seina, the honeypot was in truth a 25-year-old KGB officer, and Lonetree fell in love with her. She proceeded to use their affair to blackmail him into stealing classified documents from U.S. diplomatic offices in Moscow and in Vienna, Austria, for her so-called Uncle Sasha, also with the KGB.

Lonetree gave Sasha the names of CIA agents working deep cover in the Soviet Union and plans and blueprints for the U.S. embassies in Moscow and Vienna. Eventually overcome with guilt, Lonetree turned himself in to the CIA. Sentenced to 30 years in a military prison, his term was reduced to nine years in exchange for his cooperation. [8]

Intelligence-Gathering Methods

In business, obtaining and using information effectively is often key to gaining competitive advantage. Gathering information to compete can be accomplished ethically and legally – or not.

Ethical methods include:

— Open-source research: using the Internet, public records and previously published information

— Market analysis: using financial tools to assess information from public filings, annual reports, stockholder meeting records and the like

— Due diligence: using material provided by a company, its auditors and others who possess accurate and reliable information

— Competitive intelligence: obtaining information from any or all of the above sources and then comparing it with other information to determine strengths, weaknesses and ways to compete in a superior manner. In this way, information is transformed into intelligence.

These terms represent how companies routinely acquire information on their competitors. But what if a company wants to know more than can be obtained publicly? In such instances, the information sought could be worth millions, if not billions.

For example, a huge new building is being constructed in Kansas. There is no sign out front that announces its owner or purpose. The power company is observed installing high-tension lines. A building permit reveals the owner is Google, and it becomes evident the facility is going to be a server farm. At this point, that knowledge ceases to be called information. It becomes intelligence. This is true whether it is government, military or commercial information. You can distinguish between information and intelligence by noting that intelligence is something you do not wish your competition to know.

Trying to discern the intelligence within the information is often difficult. Some want to skip the difficult analysis and reap the benefits from intelligence quickly and easily. They resort to the unethical – and, in the United States, illegal – practices of economic or industrial espionage.

Economic versus Industrial Espionage

Although they sound somewhat alike, economic espionage differs from industrial espionage – although espionage operatives vigorously pursue them both. It's important for you to know the difference.

Economic espionage is the knowing misappropriation of trade secrets with the knowledge or intent that the offense will benefit a foreign government, foreign institution or foreign agent. Misappropriation includes, but is not limited to, stealing, copying, altering, destroying, transmitting, sending, receiving, buying, possessing or conspiring to obtain trade secrets without authorization. Section 101(a) of the Economic Espionage Act of 1996 criminalizes economic espionage.

Industrial espionage is the knowing misappropriation of trade secrets related to, or included in, a product that is produced for, or placed in, interstate or foreign commerce to the economic benefit of anyone other than the owner, with the knowledge or intent that the offense will injure the owner of that trade secret. Misappropriation includes, but is not limited to, stealing, copying, altering, destroying, transmitting, sending, receiving, buying, possessing or conspiring to misappropriate trade secrets without authorization. Industrial espionage was also criminalized under the Economic Espionage Act.

Although slightly different in definition, each can be equally damaging to the person or organization targeted for attack. The easiest way to distinguish between economic and industrial espionage is to remember that economic espionage means there is government involvement, usually a local intelligence service, although sometimes a third country. Industrial espionage is carried out without a government's assistance or involvement, usually by private collectors or business competitors.

Now that you understand what's ethical and unethical, legal and illegal, let's examine how the three types of espionage operatives conduct their nefarious activities.

The Art of Business Warfare

Most readers have heard of the teachings of Sun Tzu, the Chinese general and philosopher who wrote *The Art of War*, circa 500 B.C. The book is required reading at all U.S. military academies and most likely sits on the bookshelves of every intelligence organization in the world. Even business leaders refer to it. Remember the character Gordon Gekko in the movie *Wall Street* instructing his young protégé Bud Fox to read it? So do athletic coaches. I once witnessed Alabama head football coach Nick Saban reading it on an airplane.

Sun Tzu wrote:

"Thus, what enables the wise sovereign and the good general to strike and conquer, and achieve things beyond the reach of ordinary men, is foreknowledge. Now this foreknowledge cannot be elicited from spirits; it cannot be obtained inductively from experience, nor by any deductive calculation. Knowledge of the enemy's dispositions can only be obtained from other men." [9]

This simple fact is the basis on which every intelligence agency on the planet has been founded, and it is pervasive down to the high-school gossip level. Understanding the motivations, intentions and capabilities of an adversary and then developing a countering strategy is the most effective and efficient way to achieve victory. By employing one of the various forms of spying, a general or CEO can protect his or her organization's resources by taking advantage of his competitor's concealed weaknesses.

That is how I intend to help you, the business traveler: by teaching you how to recognize and negate the intentions of an espionage operative.

Three Key Events Driving Espionage

Economic, military and technological strength are the keys to power and influence. Since the 1970s, the battleground of the world's leading countries has been shifting from military conflict to one driven by economics. You might recall those caricatured tourists from Japan visiting the United States in the 1950s and '60s and snapping pictures of everything they saw. One reason was to gather intelligence to take home to make cheaper copies of American products. Partly as a result of those efforts, Japan rose to become the leading exporter of consumer electronics in the 1970s and '80s.

According to scholar and author Hedieh Nasheri, three world-wide events accounted for the ever-increasing emphasis on economic espionage:

The End of the Cold War   With the collapse of the Soviet Union, the spy games played by intelligence operatives shifted to the business world. The global business arena became the new playing field for spying, and the practice of economic espionage exploded.

The U.S. Court of Appeals for the Third Circuit wrote in *United States v. Hsu* (3rd Circuit, 1998) that the post-Cold War world "sent government spies scurrying to the private sector to perform illicit work for businesses and corporations, and by 1996 studies revealed that nearly $24 billion of corporate intellectual property was being stolen each year."

A Redefinition of Global Identity   Countries once defined themselves based on their military might. Today, that emphasis has shifted to economic prowess. Economic espionage allows friends to spy on friends. One nation can covertly collect economic intelligence even on an ally with less concern for reprisal than if covertly carrying out a military campaign – and that ally can do the same thing. Smaller or developing countries can likewise appropriate BI/IP without conducting expensive research and development, for which they may lack the resources, thereby accelerating their economic growth.

The Rise of the Internet   The World Wide Web – particularly through powerful search engines such as Google – offers vast opportunities for gathering open-source technological data on other countries as well as proprietary information. The rise of social media, such as LinkedIn and Facebook, along with corporate Web sites providing in-depth information about employees, products, practices and processes, constitutes a gold mine for economic espionage. Some estimates place the amount of actionable information about a competitor that can be mined from the Internet at 80 percent to 95 percent. [10]

How Does an Espionage Agent Operate?

The U.S. Office of the National Counterintelligence Executive reports that American citizens traveling abroad, whether for business or pleasure, continue to be prime targets for intelligence-collection activities. Many foreign governments and businesses place a high priority on acquiring protected information – whether classified, sensitive or proprietary – from U.S. sources.

Despite the end of the Cold War, the threat of economic and industrial espionage to Western business travelers has grown ever greater. I described the three types of espionage operatives in the previous chapter: government agents, corporate operatives and freelance private collectors. Each typically seeks different types of information, but what they obtain and the methods they use often overlap.

More problematic, an agent of espionage is not easily recognizable. True, there is the classic profile of a professional intelligence officer posing as a scientist to blend in at a symposium, and that might still take place, but now the intelligence collector sitting next to you at a symposium is more likely someone genuinely working in your field. He or she holds solid professional credentials, will ask the right questions and make correct observations. To paraphrase what the loveable comic-strip character Pogo once observed, the enemy is just like us. Moreover, as you will learn, sometimes it really is one of us.

As a business traveler, sooner or later you're going to be targeted by one or more espionage operatives – and probably they'll be using more than one method at a time. The attack will be based on what the operatives already know about you.

What could they know? Think Facebook, LinkedIn or Twitter and how much information someone could gain just from visiting or hacking those sites. It could be as little as your name, your company or your business destination. They could also have gathered more – including snapping your photo or surreptitiously taking video footage of you via cell phones and extremely tiny cameras. Your problem is you don't know who, what, when, where or how they will structure their scam, so you need to be prepared for anything.

An Operative's MO

Foreign intelligence agencies normally employ complementary and/or redundant methods of espionage. Each nation draws from its cultural heritage, political system and business practices, as well as time, manpower, funding and technical competency, to craft its espionage effort. The objective is to gather the information clandestinely, so you won't even suspect you've been a victim. That means the collector will do his or her best not to draw attention to the tactics being employed. The collector will move against you in an unobtrusive and nonthreatening fashion.

"It all starts at the airport," says my SMI security associate Pedro "Pete" Quinones, a retired U.S. Marine and intelligence officer. Indeed, in a recent Wall Street Journal article, a study revealed that 53 percent of business travelers carry sensitive information on their laptop. Of those, 65 percent admit they do not take steps to protect the data. That might be why more than 900 laptops are stolen or mislaid weekly at London's Heathrow alone. [11]

Gone through an airport without losing your laptop? That's no guarantee of security. Espionage operatives have the ability to compromise it remotely.

insider tip
In the Air with a Seasoned Business Traveler

Kenneth G. Lieberthal, Ph.D., was director of the John L. Thornton China Center and is a senior fellow in foreign policy and global economy and development at the Brookings Institution in Washington, D.C. He travels to China as often as 10 times a year, meeting with government officials, businesspeople and scholars like himself. He understands the threat to his information, so he takes the following precautions before departing on a trip:

— He uses a loaner laptop and mobile phone with their
Wi-Fi functions turned off.
— He carries a USB storage device he has made totally blank.
— He uses a virtual private network, or VPN, for connecting
to the Internet.

When he arrives in China, Dr. Lieberthal never allows his mobile phone or other electronic devices out of his sight. He does not connect to a Wi-Fi network unless his USB flash drive is

unplugged. He transfers passwords via memory from the USB device to his computer to ensure keystroke-logging software cannot detect them. [12]

Dr. Lieberthal is a seasoned traveler who understands the risks and
does everything he can to protect his valuable electronic data. His
actions are neither excessive nor paranoid. They are – or should be
– SOP for the modern business traveler. They're also, unfortunately,
only a good start.

The arsenal of foreign intelligence gathering involves more aggressive tactics, such as excessive questioning by border-control
officials, hotel-room searches and this laundry list of unnerving
techniques:

BLACKMAIL   Operatives threaten to reveal information – whether true or false – about a person to a family member, associates or
even the public unless a demand is met. Blackmail can extend to
coercion, which involves threats of physical harm or criminal pros-
ecution for the purpose of taking the person's money or property.

EXTORTION   Another form of blackmail, extortion involves taking your personal property with threat of future harm or revealing
damaging information unless you comply.

BRIBERY   As plain as it can be, this is paying you to turn over BI/
IP or in other ways act as an accomplice in intelligence gathering.
Operatives often initiate bribery because of a perceived weakness
or problem the target might be having. Most frequently, the bribe
involves money, but influence peddling is also popular. Using open-
source information, operatives can easily learn if the target is in
debt or needs money for other reasons. Perhaps his girlfriend, who
is younger than his daughter, is pregnant. The target might possess
insider-trading information. Perhaps he wants tickets to the Super
Bowl. The bribe can be as benign as paying consulting fees, in
which case picking the target's brain and pockets for valuable BI/IP
becomes an enduring source of information.

EAVESDROPPING   The practice of listening to other people's conversations to gather information can range from the strategic positioning of an unobtrusive bystander to the use of concealed audio and video recording devices.

Eavesdropping is frequently employed in social settings, where attendees feel secure and are more likely to talk about themselves and their work. It's also often used in venues such as public and host-provided transportation, restaurants, bars and meeting-facility restrooms. It's popular, because concealed devices are cost-efficient and low risk, and they can be used in conjunction with overt devices such as traffic- and pedestrian-monitoring cameras.

ELECTRONIC SURVEILLANCE AND/OR INTERCEPTION
This is the fastest-growing type of espionage MO, because it is so simple and can often be conducted at a distance, without the target ever knowing it is underway. Most prevalent are Wi-Fi intrusions, using flash drives to capture data or introduce malware, and gaining access to mobile phones, laptops and other personal electronics. Phones and computers with cameras and microphones have become particularly vulnerable, because they can be compromised to become surveillance devices – your own phone or laptop can be used to spy on you. Likewise, foreign telecommunications carriers can be untrustworthy, because most are government controlled.

Espionage operatives can also use office and hotel phones as targets, and they can monitor fax, telex and email traffic. And don't think your encrypted messages are safe; many countries have the ability to intercept and possibly break them.

ELICITATION   This is a ploy where operatives contrive a seemingly normal conversation to extract information about you, your work and your colleagues. Elicitation is subtle; it is sometimes referred to as collegiality, because operatives use it to cement a relationship with their marks. They refer to a compromised mark as an asset.

Don't confuse elicitation with direct questioning by government officials or company representatives, however. An elicitation is meant to put you at ease, so you feel comfortable sharing information. It's a preferred method, because it's difficult to recognize as an intelligence technique, and it's easily deniable by an adversary.

insider tale
Art Imitates Life
Victor Ostrovsky's book *By Way of Deception: The Making and Unmaking of a Mossad Officer* provides an excellent example of how Israeli intelligence officers were trained to perform elicitation. According to Ostrovsky, "One of the instructors turned to me and said, 'See that balcony on the third floor over there? I want you to stand here for three minutes and think. Then I want you to go to that building and within six minutes I want to see you standing on that balcony with the owner or tenant, and I want you holding a glass of water.'" That same scenario was also portrayed in the 2001 movie *Spy Game*, starring Robert Redford and Brad Pitt. [13]

INTRUSIONS   These involve actions such as covertly entering an office, hotel room, secure area or electronic equipment location to steal or make reproductions of documents, magnetic and audio-video media, and/or install electronic eavesdropping equipment.

Although most intrusions are surreptitious, American travelers have reported returning to their hotel rooms to find their belongings searched or evidence of unnecessary maintenance activities.

Other reported incidents of intrusion include:
— Laptops showing signs of unauthorized use or actual damage
— Packages that have been opened and resealed or left open
— Locks on briefcases and suitcases missing or showing signs of tampering
— Theft of the aforementioned items

In all likelihood, these activities were acts of espionage conducted by the host government, an intelligence service or business operatives in the country you are visiting. Operatives frequently receive cooperation from hotel staff. You can't always tell if your privacy has been compromised, but as in **Rule 1**, it's always prudent to assume you're under surveillance via cameras, microphones or the operatives themselves.

Several countries, and possibly foreign companies, have developed the ability to overcome commercial computer intrusion-protection software and hardware. If you detect and report them, they can be explained away as a criminal activity; for example, some unauthorized person looking for passports, cash and other valuables.

You should expect that officials will take no action to locate the thieves – proof positive that an ounce of prevention is worth a pound of cure.

MISDIRECTION   You must know by now that it's unadvisable to take sensitive information with you on an electronic device, especially to foreign destinations. Yet another reason is the practice of misdirection. It originated in stage magic, where the magician distracts the audience or a subject into looking away during a trick. Pickpockets commonly try to distract or intimidate their prey to make their task easier. No one was better at this than the magician Tony Slydini, who could reduce his victims to stupefaction.

Using misdirection, operatives can conceal valuable BI/IP in non-associated files – for example, MP3 music files, photo images or smartphone app shells that do nothing. Another imaginative ploy is renaming BI/IP files with dull-sounding names and burying them in unlikely directories.

Varied and creative forms of misdirection emerged shortly after 9/11. As U.S. security at airports cracked down, resentful countries began harassing American travelers by detaining them and taking away their electronic gear to be examined and scanned, so operatives could copy or download the data. Again, if you carry BI/IP on an electronic device such as a laptop, you must never allow this to happen. Refuse to be separated from your device, even if it means forfeiting entry into the country.

PHYSICAL ATTACKS   Such incidents have become rare, because of the ease of using electronic means, but assaults still occur. In all such cases, the assault was perpetrated to obtain intelligence. The most common types are:
  — Kidnapping, either the target or a family member
  — Drugging, often with a truth serum or sedative
  — Torture, sometimes physical but more often psychological, with women travelers subjected to sexual contact or rape

Most espionage operatives have abandoned physical assaults, because they are not as productive or efficient as electronic methods. Nevertheless, it's common for them to use multiple methods, sometimes as a planned approach but more often to see if one method works then switch to another if it doesn't.

Espionage is often a silent and invisible crime. That said, don't allow yourself to assume it isn't happening or that it can't happen to you. It is and it could.

Never forget **Rule 1**: Assume at all times you are being surveilled by someone who wants your information.

The stakes are high, and for the espionage operative the rewards are great.

insider tale
Spreading the Word
Much like the Department of Homeland Security's "See Something, Say Something" awareness campaign, which encourages U.S. citizens watch out for possible terrorist activity, the FBI began a nine-city billboard campaign in 2012 to "Protect America's trade Secrets" from espionage-related behavior.

4. Why should you care if someone surreptitiously enters your hotel room and downloads your computer's hard drive – particularly if all it contains are innocuous spreadsheets, a couple of sales presentations and maybe some episodes of Mad Men you downloaded for the flight?

I've heard many business travelers express nonchalance about hotel intrusions. What they forget is that access to their laptop and mobile phone doesn't end with copying hard drives or hacking SIM cards or memory sticks. An operative who gets that far will likely install a worm and/or keystroke logger, allowing access to the company's servers back home anytime the espionage sponsor wishes. In other words, not only the individual traveler but also all of the organization's information can be deeply – and often irrevocably – compromised.

5. What about those overweight, underappreciated, low-ranking sales reps working for a manufacturing company and flying to a trade show? They don't carry business secrets or anything important to their company. Why would an operative want to stalk individuals at that level?

It's precisely because they're underappreciated that a competitor or intelligence service would try to compromise them. The two key ingredients to recruiting a competitor's employees are access and motivation. Many employees have access to more than they think. If operatives spot a potential motivation – such as a company rep who feels underappreciated – they will target that person and work that feeling to their advantage. They will attempt to exploit the mark by persuading him or her to reveal information about their organization in exchange for money, sexual favors or a perceived increase in prestige. By accepting the offer, the mark becomes a competitor's asset.

6. If economic and industrial espionage really happen, why aren't they reported regularly in the news media?

It does indeed happen, far more frequently than you think. The reason it doesn't often appear in the media is it's difficult to detect. Also, because of the embarrassment involved, companies and government agencies don't like to admit they've been victimized – just as they don't want it known they've been hacked. Likewise, when operatives steal BI/IP from business travelers' laptops, their companies tend not to blab about the losses. The problem is such reluctance makes it difficult to keep travelers aware of the hazards, and it's therefore easier for operatives to continue their activities.

7. Are popular, franchised hotels overseas any safer than lesser-known or independent establishments?

Unfortunately, many popular hotels overseas are locally owned and operated. Often, the local government will use a private citizen as a cover to purchase the hotel, while the host intelligence service sets up operations inside. Moreover, even the most reputable chain hotels can harbor maids, bellmen, clerks and others who are also on the payroll of competitors or intelligence services.

8. With the end of the Cold War, doesn't most of the spying occur over the Internet via hacking and phishing?

That's partially correct. Internet spying is huge, but you might be shocked to learn there are more spies in Washington, D.C., than any other city in the world. In fact, the U.S. intelligence community believes there are more Russian intelligence officers working in the United States now than there were back in the 1980s. Their target has shifted, however, from capturing military intelligence to hunting for business technology.

Need to know more?
Email us: questions@among-enemies.com

3. How to Think and Act Like a Counterintelligence Officer

"Counterintelligence embraces both 'information gathered' and 'activities conducted' to counter foreign intelligence threats. Counterintelligence provides an ability to protect sensitive national security information and to prevent the loss of critical technological, industrial, and commercial information."

– From the CIA's Web site

Proactive, Defensive, Business Counter-Espionage

Once, as a young intelligence officer, I was sent on a short assignment – known as temporary duty or TDY – to Africa. It's the perfect place to cut your teeth while attempting covert/clandestine operations. If you screw up in Africa, you can usually pay someone off to make your mistakes go away.

I can't discuss my assignment, of course, but I recall that my return flight to the United States was routed through Casablanca, Morocco. I had never been to this legendary city before, so I was eager to see if it actually resembled the 1943 Humphrey Bogart movie of the same name – in terms of its amalgam of cultures and intrigue, not its similarity to the Warner Bros. studio back lot.

As luck would have it, my hotel was a popular European chain located within walking distance to Rick's Café, a tourist restaurant run by Americans on Rue Sour Jdid. I enjoyed a delicious meal in the replica setting, although the pianist with the requisite name of Sam was Arab.

When I returned to my hotel, about two hours later, to my great surprise I found my room had been ransacked. My suitcases had been emptied onto the floor, the room safe opened and all my electronics stolen – my laptop, extra cell phone, iPod and video camera.

I immediately called the front desk and demanded they contact the police to file a report. A lone police officer soon appeared. He apologized, stating he was ill-equipped to perform an investigation and preferred that the hotel handle the matter internally. He departed within 10 minutes.

Taking matters into my own hands, I noticed there were closed-circuit security cameras at the hotel entrance. I insisted that the manager show me the video footage from the past two hours. He informed me that I was not allowed into their security office, but he would personally review the tape and get back to me. After 20 minutes he returned and said no other individuals had entered or exited the hotel since I left for dinner.

Furious, I checked out the next morning for my flight home without my personal belongings. Naturally, the hotel refused to reimburse me for anything and charged me full price for my room. After multiple threatening letters to the parent chain, I have yet to receive so much as an apology.

At least the hotel people didn't declare they were "shocked, shocked" that a theft had occurred.

Was the deed perpetrated by hotel personnel? Possibly. But more likely the local intelligence service had identified me as a competitor at the airport and placed me under surveillance. As soon as I departed for dinner, they exploited my room for any useful information.

I was lucky. Nothing stolen contained government-related information or anything to do with my assignment. If it had, it might have caused an international incident.

It was a hard lesson to learn, but one I hope you will take to heart: Never, ever, leave your electronics unattended in your hotel room.

I also hope by now you understand how vulnerable you are to espionage as you travel the world. You, the business traveler, are a prime target for operatives, even if you're traveling domestically but especially internationally. You must protect yourself and your BI/IP by all reasonable means to help guard your company's competitive advantage.

That said, are you ready to learn how to think and act like a counterintelligence officer?

As I mentioned earlier, this doesn't require transforming you into a James Bond. You won't be taking overt action against foreign operatives, and you won't be disabling any surveillance equipment.

You're going to become more observant and careful in all your actions and interactions while traveling.

You're going to raise your risk-awareness level.

You'll learn to recognize potentially sticky encounters and situations for what they are, and you'll be able to protect yourself.

You'll also be able to do these things mindfully, defensively and without drawing attention to yourself.

I travel all the time for business – incidentally, earning Global Services status as one of the top 1 percent of spenders on United Airlines several years in a row – and I know how tough the ocean-hopping life can be. It isn't just the crisscrossing of time zones and the constant jetlag, or the airplane food and wine that leave your stomach in knots. Or the craving for creature comforts such as a hot shower, some good food and restful sleep. It's that the last thing you, as an exhausted traveler, want to think about on entering a hotel room is securing your laptop or worrying about the threat of electronic devices embedded in the ceiling.

The problem is that your vulnerability to espionage is a constant threat. In fact, your ignorance of the threat increases the risk.

How vulnerable are you? Try this 10-question, true-or-false quiz:

T / F   When traveling, you never leave your laptop unattended, even on your airplane seat, hotel room, the gym or when you go out dining or sightseeing.

T / F   You have never downloaded a file to your computer from someone other than an authorized colleague in your organization.

T / F   You have never had a sensitive or confidential work conversation in the business lounge of an airport or in your hotel room.

T / F   You have never been approached by a complete stranger in a foreign country, or en route to a foreign country, who asked you intrusive questions about your business.

T / F   You have developed a cover story and/or prepared a response in case you encounter an over-inquisitive seatmate.

T / F   You carry a sanitized travel laptop and mobile phone on international business trips, and you get updated passwords and SIM cards/memory sticks for each overseas trip you make.

T / F   Prior to an overseas trip, you establish secure communication protocols and designated code words for conveying sensitive BI/IP in phone calls, electronic messages and other forms of communication to your office.

T / F   Your organization has security training, policies and procedures in place to educate and remind its business travelers continually about the threats of economic and industrial espionage.

T / F   Your organization has a policy established that requires its travelers to report suspicious activity as well as a database that documents and tracks this activity.

T / F   Your organization has a system in place to determine employee susceptibility to bribery and/or blackmail.

How did you do? If you checked **T** for all 10 questions, congratulations! You should be complimented for your outstanding operational security practices – OPSEC in our parlance. If you answered **F** to any of the questions, however, your organization could be vulnerable – a flaw that could cost you dearly in currency as well as lost opportunities and even business failure due to competitive disadvantage. It happens every day.

With this basic understanding of your exposure, let's go into more depth.

The Business Traveler's Checklist

You learned the why, who and how of economic and industrial espionage in Chapter 2. Now, here are the whys and hows of *counter*-espionage – with you as the who.

Let's start by listing the five wheres; places you are at risk of espionage:

— At the airport
— On the plane
— In the taxi
— In the hotel
— At the meeting or conference

Here are five short, illustrative stories to explain how you can deploy counter-espionage techniques each location.

Counter-Espionage at the Airport

Alicia, a business-development executive for an alternative-energy company in California, is on her way to a meeting in Madrid. She becomes a victim of doxing, or gathering information about a person from online sources, while using the free Wi-Fi network at a San Francisco International airport café.

This is how it happens:
Alicia asks a woman sitting at the table next to her if she will watch her bags while she gets a cup of coffee. An espionage operative, the woman slips a flash drive into Alicia's laptop as soon as she is out of sight. The drive contains a malware program that will begin capturing her email messages. Once the woman has acquired Alicia's identity, she can learn her destination and pass the information along to a Spanish operative who tails Alicia from Madrid-Barajas International Airport to her hotel. Other operatives arrange to assign Alicia a suite that is bugged for audio and video, and via the hotel Wi-Fi they can monitor her email exchanges.

This is only the beginning of Alicia's troubles. One of the messages she downloads contains a keystroke-capture program, so everything she types from then on will be compromised.

This scenario is repeated frequently at busy international airports. As I've explained, espionage operatives can work for government intelligence services, multinational corporations or private collectors. Whoever hires them, it's certain you will unwittingly pass by them in the terminal. Many lurk in the airline lounges, dutifully searching for opportunities to strike up a conversation with an unwitting business traveler. Some prefer to eavesdrop near ticket counters. Often, they have already learned who you are and are attempting to discover where you're going. Others look for arriving business travelers just outside the security area.

Your job is to thwart their efforts. Here's how:
— From the moment you arrive at an airport, assume you're under surveillance by someone – once again, **Rule 1**. It might be airport security, law enforcement, intelligence services, business competitors or espionage operatives. These days, closed-circuit TV camera coverage is extensive at airports, even in seemingly poor or under-resourced countries. You need to become as innocuous as

possible – or, as they say in the intelligence community, be boring.

insider tip
Leave It to the Pros
Never do anything that a surveillance team assigned to monitor your activities would consider suspicious. This includes spy trade-craft, Hollywood-style, such as using a storefront window in the terminal as a mirror to detect possible surveillance behind you.

Another amateurish example involves walking around a cor-ner and stopping suddenly to try to catch someone who has been following you.

As a businessperson, if you start playing spy games with a foreign intelligence service, you're asking for trouble. Be alert, but don't be stupid. You're not trained to do field tradecraft.

On the inside you may be on high alert, but on the outside your demeanor should reflect that of an everyday business trav-eler.

Again, be boring.

— If you park your vehicle at the airport, the security and/or parking enforcement people will probably record your license plate number. This has become common practice in the United States, for example. Airport parking opens the door for an operative to moni-tor or tag your car and determine how long you are away. Consider taking a taxi – it's less obvious.

— When checking in for your flight, if other travelers are stand-ing within earshot, lower your voice when you speak to the ticket clerk. Slide your printed reservation or itinerary across the count-er face down. Cover your passport with a plain passport wallet to avoid identifying your country of origin.

— Disguise your identity on your luggage identification tag. Use an abbreviated name or reverse your order: For example, instead of "Brian Williams," use "Will B." Don't use your business card, and use a tag with a protective cover to conceal the information from the eyes of strangers.

— Don't wear a shirt or hat or carry a briefcase that identi-fies your employer, and leave your country-of-origin flag pins and patches at home.

— Don't disclose your destination to strangers. Anyone, no matter how innocent-looking, could be an operative. If someone asks, "Where are you flying off to today?" instead of saying "Cairo" or "London" simply say "Africa" or "the U.K." Bear in mind that if the individual is an undercover law-enforcement or intelligence officer, lying could be more dangerous than telling the truth. Be vague but honest when asked about your travel. Redirect or shrug off questions when someone you do not know tries to engage you.

— Avoid transporting electronic devices and sensitive corporate materials in checked baggage. In the United States, the Transportation Security Administration can open any bag, and baggage handlers are notorious for theft. Remember also that luggage locks are no protection.

— Avoid using the Wi-Fi service in an airport business lounge or public seating area – any public Wi-Fi, for that matter. In many instances, the service is either being compromised by espionage operatives or provided by an organization affiliated with the host government and its intelligence service.

— Likewise, avoid it on the plane. On board Wi-Fi is especially vulnerable to monitoring by other passengers. Airline-provided Internet firewalls are not secure. Any sensitive emails you might be typing up in business class could possibly be read by a guy sitting back in seat 42C.

— If you must use the Internet to communicate while traveling, don't use your real name or personal email or your company's email system. Instead, do one of two things:

1. Set up a disposable email address with a free provider such as Gmail, Hotmail or Yahoo, and use a vague login.

2. Better yet, install a secure email program, such as a Web-based email service with Pretty Good Privacy (PGP) encryption or a domain-based service that provides near-total isolation and security.

We'll discuss this again in Chapter 5.

Regarding user names on one of the free services, instead of something like jane.businessperson@xyzcompany.com, use a handle that's counterintuitive, such as abc19msu@hotmail.com. Change the password after every leg of your trip or business meeting, and follow the guidelines for a maximum-strength password using a combination of letters, numbers and characters. Use only this account while traveling, and deactivate it on your computer and phone before boarding your return flight.

Your recipients should also use an alias email account. You don't want to go to the trouble of establishing a disposable email address, only to have operatives discover you sent something to your company or boss using the corporate email – which can happen inadvertently if you copy emails to other parties. Keep your communications as nonproprietary as possible.

— Avoid using complimentary or public computers in an airport lounge or public place. It's extremely easy for an operative to install keystroke-capture software or insert a flash drive in an unseen USB port to record your online activities. Consider who owns the airport lounge and the network. In many cases, it isn't a legally liable private company but rather the host government.

— If you must communicate by email or phone while in the business lounge, establish code words with the person on the other end in order to disguise your conversation or disinterest others in eavesdropping. For example, instead of saying or writing, "We just signed a two-million-dollar deal with Apple Computer!" you could say "AC just invited us to dinner. He said he's got 2 steaks on the grill."

Use your imagination to come up with your own coded language, but avoid getting too creative. Once again, boring is best. I once heard a story about two dotcom entrepreneurs who used the fictitious Klingon language from the Star Trek series to hold secure communications. Imagine overhearing that conversation in an airport lounge – talk about suspicious.

— When you travel for business, consider purchasing a prepaid cell phone. Many commercial software applications can easily track your position and movements using cell tower triangulation. If you regularly rotate out your phone (and not just your SIM card), you will make it considerably more difficult for competitors to pinpoint your location or learn your calling habits. Do this and you'll make it difficult for an operative to build a profile on you.

Rimington's Laptop
Even the best forget the basics sometimes. In June 2012, Dame
Stella Rimington, the former director general of MI5 – England's
internal intelligence agency – was traveling through London's
Heathrow International Airport when her laptop was stolen. Video suggests she seems to have left the laptop in the top compartment of her bag, which was removed when she stepped away
momentarily from her luggage trolley. Publicly it was reported
that the laptop held only research for her new book. Unofficial-
ly, however, authorities worried that the laptop contained contact information of former colleagues still active. Most likely, the
thief had no idea from whom he or she was stealing, but there is
no way of knowing who the final recipient was. It is safe to say
that even a former government intelligence official's personal
laptop would be a valuable commodity to any foreign spy agency or private collector. Rimington, 77, served as the first female
director of MI5 from 1992 to 1996. It is widely speculated that
her nomination inspired the casting of Judi Dench as the tough-
talking spy chief "M" in the recent James Bond movies.

Aboard the Airplane

Say you've survived the espionage risks in the airport, or perhaps the
train station if traveling by rail – the principles are the same. Now
you're aboard the plane, sitting in your comfortable, business-class
seat. If you think you're safe from intrusions and infiltrations, please
flip back to the Introduction and read it again.

The truth is that once you've fastened your seatbelt for the flight,
an experienced espionage operative has you cornered. In all likelihood, he or she already knows who you are, whom you work for,
even perhaps the nature of your business trip. Ever since commercial
air travel began, spies have used the excuse of a long, transoceanic
flight as an opportunity to acquaint themselves with an unknowing
target.

So, the next time you're whiling away the hours on an airliner:

— Don't feel obligated to engage in conversations initiated by
strangers. You don't have to be rude; accept that small talk is a natural part of the travel experience. But set a polite boundary with

something like, "I've been working for 72 hours straight, and I need to just rest quietly on this flight." If your seatmate's questions persist or get too personal, put on your headset and watch the movie.

— For that matter, avoid discussing business altogether while in flight, particularly aboard a foreign airliner. Even if you aren't overheard by an operative, your conversation could be monitored.

insider tale
The (Airliner's) Walls Have Ears

In 1981, Pierre Marion, then director of French intelligence – the Direction Générale de la Sécurité Extérieure, or DGSE – established a 20-agent branch to spy on U.S. high-technology companies. Nearly a decade after creating the unit, Marion proudly told the French newsmagazine L'Express that "France had planted audio devices in the first-class cabins of [state-owned] Air France flights."

Later that year, he told Newsweek magazine that "the DGSE directed its efforts toward American computer and electronics companies, including IBM, Texas Instruments and Corning;" companies in competition with the French-owned state enterprise Groupe Bull, which at the time was struggling to gain market share against its American rivals.

As Marion went on to admit, "The program was not directed [only] against the United States, but was worldwide." A spokesman for Air France categorically denied the allegations, the French Foreign Ministry refused to comment on the story, and Marion later retracted his comments. [14]

Nevertheless, it really happened.

— Avoid drinking too much alcohol on flights. This is a given for any situation, but when the glasses are repeatedly refilled, just remember the old adage, "Loose lips sink ships." Limit your alcohol consumption to one or two glasses, preferably during a meal, to avoid letting your guard down.

— Shield your passwords and computer screen from those around you; use different passwords abroad than you use on your office computer. Privacy screen protectors also work well to keep prying eyes from peeking at your monitor.

— If you get up to use the lavatory, take your computer with you – seriously! If you think that's taking things too far, put it back in its case and fasten the zipper handles with zip ties. But use zip ties with serial numbers – because these people think of everything.

— If you plan to sleep, especially if you'll be wearing a sleep mask and earplugs, consider moving your briefcase and computer bag under your feet. You might even want to clutch them to your chest. When the lights go out, and everyone in business class is thoroughly sedated by red wine or sleeping pills, it's relatively easy for an operative to search your stowed belongings in the overhead compartment. An experienced operative can exploit your laptop and cell phone and rifle your briefcase for sensitive documents in moments, all while you're snoozing. Later, when you awaken, you will never know the guy sitting across the aisle from you has read your email messages and copied that all-important business plan saved on your hard drive.

— Prior to landing, confirm that your sensitive belongings – laptop, cell phone, notebook, music player, passport, documents, wallet, etc. – are all where they should be.

— While you're completing your landing card (the immigration/ customs form), be sure the person sitting next to you isn't reading your personal information. This form typically indicates where you are going, your hotel, where you came from, what you have purchased and the purpose of your trip. That information is nobody's business but yours – and the customs and immigration officer's.

In the Taxi

You've had your coffee and taken advantage of the refreshing hot towel to wipe the sleep from your eyes. The airplane is on the ground, and you have successfully navigated through immigration/ customs and baggage claim.

Now, it's time to make your way through the airport to find a taxi to your hotel. Preferably, you want to have a prearranged, private driver meet you when you land; one who, along with his company, has been fully vetted by your organization's security department. When you approach the driver, each of you should use a prearranged identifying sign that does not expose you or your company affiliation. Use a code word or phrase to verify each other's identity.

Given that most business travelers don't receive the royal driver-and-limo treatment when they land, let's discuss taxi security using this hypothetical situation based on fact:

Josh and Katie are New York investment bankers who have flown from Geneva to Istanbul as part of a prospective real estate deal. They hail a taxi outside Ataturk Airport and instruct the driver, "Take us to the Four Seasons, please." With an embarrassed smile, the driver replies in the rearview mirror, "I sorry. My English no good. Four Seasons Hotel, yeah?"

"Yes, the Four Seasons Hotel," Josh replies.

As they drive through the winding streets of Istanbul, Josh and Katie discuss the details of their real-estate venture without fear of the driver eavesdropping. Soon thereafter, they're on a conference call with their firm's managing partner in Manhattan, discussing negotiation strategies.

As the taxi pulls up to the Four Seasons, Josh hands the driver a wad of Turkish lira and walks away. With a big grin, the driver responds with an awkward, "Tenk you." Now alone, the driver makes a call on his cell phone and in perfect English states the following:

"Yes, sir, the two Americans have just checked into the hotel. They are going to move forward with the project; however, they intend to counteroffer on price and percentage of ownership. They had a conference call with New York while they were in the cab. Don't worry. I have the entire conversation recorded."

It should come as no surprise that taxis have been used for decades by intelligence services and criminals alike to entrap unsuspecting travelers. Many government services post surveillance teams at airports utilizing their own taxis. Their sole intent is to keep tabs on targeted businesspeople. An experienced team will lure the mark into one of their taxis then attempt to build rapport and elicit information.

Follow these tips to avoid becoming a victim of espionage while riding in a taxi:

— Even if the driver claims not to speak your language, don't assume he's telling the truth. Many drivers pretend not to understand you so they can eavesdrop on your conversations with other travelers or on the phone.

— Be cautious anytime some taxis pass you by and one unexpectedly stops for you. This could mean the other drivers have been instructed to stay away because someone has targeted you, either an operative or a criminal element.

— Be sure the taxi driver's name and cab number are visible. Confirm that the photo matches the driver. If the ID isn't visible, or the face doesn't match the photo, the driver might not want his real identity known. Make sure the meter is running, too.

— Always have the name of your destination and its location written in the local language in case your taxi driver truly does not speak your language.

— Avoid announcing the name of your hotel or destination loud enough to be heard by anyone standing nearby.

— Carry a street map with the highlighted route your taxi should take. Or, less preferable, follow along with your smartphone's GPS navigation. Just know, however, if you use that feature it will allow your movements to be tracked.

— Make sure the taxi doesn't deviate from this route, and know where you are at all times. If the driver starts to deviate, question him immediately, or insist that he pull over so you can find another cab.

— If the driver begins asking questions, do not disclose the purpose of your visit. Again, have a cover story prepared – for example, you're attending a wedding. It's always better to tell a half-truth instead of a flat-out lie. You never know when you might be challenged about your previous claims at a later point during your trip. Wedding? Between your firm and your foreign partner, of course.

— If you're concerned about the driver knowing your final destination, divert him. Give him the address of another hotel near your own, and walk your real destination after he has departed.

— In many countries, the taxi driver will attempt to befriend you and offer to be your personal driver for the duration. Avoid this trap.

It's a common way for outsiders to keep tabs on your travel schedule and destinations.

— Vary your travel times as much as possible. Operatives watch for patterns, so don't leave the hotel at, say, 9 o'clock sharp every morning.

— If the same taxi driver picks you up twice during your business trip, in all likelihood it's no coincidence. You've either become targeted by espionage operatives or, worse, the soon-to-be victim of a crime.

In the Hotel

You've made it safely to the hotel and are now preparing to check in, savoring the sanctuary of your room and a hot shower. But don't let your guard down. The threat of espionage is just beginning.

Hotels are the number-one location for foreign intelligence services and business competitors to spy on you. You are at their mercy. The surveillance team will attempt to monitor your every move with cleverly hidden audio and video devices. The bellboys, maids and valets will search your belongings whenever you are gone. Not to mention, a hotel room is the perfect setting for a blackmail scenario or, as in as in the following case, a setup for theft.

Troy is a newbie business traveler who has just checked into his hotel in a popular South American city. There, he's greeted by a friendly, English-speaking desk clerk who asks for his passport and, seemingly innocuously, the nature of his business. Troy discloses he will be meeting with one of the most prominent building contractors in the country. This seems to impress the clerk greatly, and he wishes Troy a most productive visit.

In his room, Troy is unknotting his tie when he hears a knock at the door. He opens it to find two stunningly beautiful women standing in the hallway. They explain in broken English they are gifts from the company he is there to visit and wish to provide him with "astonishing pleasures."

Flattered and titillated, Troy invites them in then excuses himself to the bathroom to calm his nerves and prepare for what lies ahead. A few minutes later, when he opens the bathroom door, the two women have disappeared along with his laptop, briefcase, mobile phone, passport and wallet. Formerly stirred and now shaken, Troy sits down to figure out how he can explain to his boss what happened.

Follow these steps to ensure you don't become a victim of espionage or entrapment in your hotel:

— Be aware of others standing nearby when you check in. Avoid saying your name out loud or chatting about your stay or disclosing other personal matters with the desk clerk.

— Don't show your passport to anyone who is not authorized to inspect it.

— When providing your guest information, be circumspect. Don't give your home phone number or specific details about your home address. If the desk clerk asks for your business card, say you left them in your checked luggage. Often, the clerk will pass along your business card and registration information to the country's intelligence service.

— Some international hotels require you to surrender your passport when checking in so they can make a photocopy. They might tell you they will return it sometime later. You should insist that they photocopy it in your presence. If they claim the copy machine is broken, instruct them to call you when it's fixed.

One reason why local authorities attempt to examine your passport is your visa stamps, which can help them build a profile on you. Don't be fooled by this information-collection exercise by the hotel – they are cooperating with individuals or agencies seeking intelligence. A simple remedy to relinquishing your passport is to hand the clerk a photocopy of your identification page you have already made yourself.

— Don't allow the bellman to take your luggage up to your room without you. That will give him the chance to take it away in a separate elevator and stop on the way up to dig through it, because it doesn't take long for an experienced operative to search your belongings and return them to you.

— When you arrive at your room, notice if the rooms in which you and your colleagues are staying are stacked in a corner, one above the next; for example, if you've been assigned rooms 104, 204, 304. If so, there's a good chance the rooms have been fitted with electronic surveillance gear, because corner rooms make it easy to run wires up and down the outside of the building unnoticed.

— Can someone watch your door easily from across the hall? Be suspicious if that room always shows a DO NOT DISTURB sign. Operatives might be monitoring your comings and goings.

insider tip
Here's Not Looking at You
If you have a peephole on your hotel room door, remember that a device called a peephole reverser, originally created by law enforcement tactical teams, can be used to monitor activity inside your room. This was how ESPN sideline reporter Erin Andrews was unknowingly videotaped in the nude. Always cover your peephole with tape or at least a piece of tissue paper.

— Most hotel rooms have a door connecting to one of the adjacent rooms. If so, make sure you block that door with furniture or luggage. It's much easier and more discrete for a surveillance team to enter your room through the connecting door than risk being observed entering from the hall.

— Always assume your hotel room is under audio and video surveillance – but never look for surveillance devices in your room. If you are seen on camera poking around for such gear – or, worse, you happen to find something – the local intelligence service will probably make the remainder of your trip uncomfortable. For example, if you go looking for devices, you could be accused of being a spy. Don't ever put yourself in that position.

— Never engage with strangers who come knocking on your door at odd hours of the day or night. There's a reason espionage operatives arrange sexual advances toward business travelers: They frequently work. If you value your job, your family, your reputation and your life, you only need to remember one word: blackmail. Follow this time-tested advice: Don't do anything on a business trip, especially in your hotel room, that you would not want to see published on the front page of your local newspaper.

— Never assume your valuables are secure in the hotel room safe. All hotel safes can be opened in seconds with a master key or code, often by your housekeeper. By keeping your valuables there, you have provided everything the espionage operative seeks in a single location.

I once checked into a hotel in Bangkok only to find that the room safe had been accidently locked by the previous guest. The bellboy came up and pressed in the numbers 0000# and the safe magically opened. When I questioned him about it, he said many people make that mistake, so every safe in the hotel could be opened with the same code.

— If you leave your electronic devices unattended for more than 15 minutes, assume they have been compromised. If you don't want your information imaged or copied, you cannot let them out of your sight.

— Anything you send electronically – whether by fax, PDA, computer or cell phone – can probably be intercepted from within your hotel room. Wireless transmissions are especially vulnerable.

— Terminate your Internet connections when not in use. Disable Wi-Fi, infrared (IR), Bluetooth ports and other features you do not need. Clear and shut down your browser after each use, and delete your browsing history, cookies and temporary Internet files. Don't use the password-storage feature when logging into Web sites.

— Use a piece of electrical or other opaque tape to cover the camera on your laptop when not in use. It can be covertly and re-motely activated to monitor you and your surroundings.

— Never use the computers in the hotel's business center to send emails, search for sensitive information, or check your social-media accounts. That's where keystroke-capture software is most likely in-stalled.

— As James Bond's nemesis Goldfinger once said, "Once is hap-penstance. Twice is coincidence. The third time it's enemy action." Be alert to people you repeatedly see in the hotel lobby. This is how most surveillance teams acquire their targets. Knowing your behavior patterns, they can follow you or search your room while you're absent. The intelligence field uses a saying more emphatic than Fleming's: "There are no coincidences."

—— If you spend time in a hotel bar, be cautious of what you say and to whom. They're prime hunting grounds for espionage operatives.

—— If you do have a few drinks, watch each one as it's being made, or accept drinks only from bottles that are opened in front of you. The number of international business travelers who have had their drinks spiked with drugs is legion – including yours truly, when I fell victim to a spiked drink in a Baltic country. Before travelers realize what has happened, they are being taken to their room by their new "friends," thus opening the door, literally, to all sorts of espionage issues.

—— Have you ever heard the saying, "If you're not attractive back home, you're not attractive when you're away?" Believe it. If you're approached by a gorgeous individual of the opposite sex (or the same sex, as the case may be), assume you're being targeted.

insider tip
Low-Tech Counter-Espionage from the Old School

I was fortunate in my career to work with some highly regarded, and highly decorated, intelligence officers, and they had developed some ingeniously simple ways of detecting surveillance. One such skilled officer was Wil, who became not only a good friend but also a great mentor.

Wil and I were having breakfast one morning in a hotel restaurant, when I noticed him taking a handful of Rice Krispies from his cereal bowl and placing them in his pocket. I asked him what he was doing and he replied that he suspected someone had been entering his room while he was out each day – even after he had hung the DO NOT DISTURB sign on the door. He said he would place the Rice Krispies under the floor mat in front of the desk in his room. If the grains were crushed when he returned, he'd know someone had been there.

Another tip I learned from the old-timers: You can't be too discreet when you travel. Don't even give your true name to a local dry cleaner, lest the cleaner writes that name on your laundry tags.

At the Meeting or Conference

You have flown halfway around the world, and nothing adverse has happened. Now it is time for your business meeting, followed by a walk through the trade-show floor at the convention center. You're ready to engage your potential clients in negotiation. You're on their turf, so you have to stay sharp. Your company's future is at stake, and you can't let the threat of espionage blow it for you. Take Ted's case, for example.

Ted, an American venture capitalist, attends a conference and trade show in Europe, where he is seeking investment opportunities. A pretty hostess in a company booth approaches him and offers a free version of their exciting software application. She says she can install it on his laptop in seconds from the USB flash drive on the lanyard resting between her breasts.

Ted takes a look at the device, and its location, but he balks, suspecting it contains a virus. The woman assures him it's safe and promises to give him the flash drive afterward. She tugs on it and playfully adds there are some photos of her on it as well. Ted raises his hands to the tops of her shoulders and removes the lanyard, saying he will install the program later and return her flash drive when she joins him for a drink in the hotel bar at the end of the day. The woman suddenly turns speechless.

Back in his suite, Ted plugs the flash drive into his bare-bones traveling laptop. As he examines the file directory, the light on the flash drive begins blinking, indicating it is automatically installing a program. Ted quickly discerns its purpose is to mirror the contents of his laptop then probably log onto the hotel Wi-Fi network to send his information to a remote server. But his laptop has no Wi-Fi capability, so the program is aborted.

Ted takes the flash drive and his laptop to the conference security center. Then he returns to the booth, accompanied by a guard, but the hostess has disappeared.

Follow these simple rules, and you should be able to take the plane home with yourself and your BI/IP intact:

— If you're waiting in the client's lobby with your business partner or colleagues, don't discuss your negotiating or presentation strategy. Many businesses install cameras and audio devices in their waiting areas to probe their guests' conversations prior to an important meeting.

— Understand the concept of elicitation, as described on page 40, and learn how to avoid answering your foreign host's probing questions. Take a lesson from the ever-polite and often-evasive Asian negotiating techniques. For example, be wary if your client insists that you sign a document before negotiations can continue. A common intelligence tactic is to tell foreigners they must sign bogus documents – usually disguised as nondisclosure agreements or acceptance of some international business regulation. Companies also often use this device as a test to see how a prospective foreign business partner will react. Chances are, if you have traveled a long distance, you probably will feel obligated to comply to avoid returning home empty-handed.

What you might not realize, however, is that by signing you have ceded some control over your negotiating power and allowed your opponent to gauge your susceptibility to influence and/or possible future bribery.

Don't sign anything that isn't a completed contract – ever. If your client insists, reply that you will take the document home for the authorized individual to sign. Always be respectful of your hosts, but remain skeptical of their underlying intentions and motivations.

— When hosting sensitive business meetings at your own location, ask your employees, business partners and guests to remove the batteries from their cell phones. This will mitigate the threat of roving bugs or their internal microphones being covertly activated so they can secretly record the meeting. Some companies require that cell phones and laptops be left outside the conference room or with the receptionist.

— Never leave your laptop unattended. After giving a dynamic PowerPoint presentation, your host might say, "Let's go to lunch. You can leave your things here. I will lock the room." If so, apologize and insist it is against your company's security policy. Remember, it would be very easy to keep you away as long as necessary to copy your hard drive or install malware or a keystroke logger.

— Although some cultures find it perfectly acceptable to drink – sometimes heavily – at lunch or dinner, resist the urge to keep pace with your foreign hosts. If you're invited to an event where you suspect heavy drinking will occur, be sure to eat a hearty meal either before or during the ceremony. Milk or greasy foods will help coat your stomach. Some former case officers I know will even take a swig of olive oil before heading out for the evening. Take tiny sips throughout the night to give the impression of drinking more than you actually are. Substitute sparkling water with lime for a cocktail. Try to drink two glasses of water for every glass of alcohol.

— Resist flirting with or making advances toward attractive associates your hosts introduce. Again, this is often a test to determine your susceptibility to blackmail and bribery.

— If you attend a trade show, do not accept gifts from vendors, such as USB flash drives, downloads or even DVDs, or allow them to be installed on your electronic devices.

— Remember, espionage operatives love international trade shows and conventions, so be cautious about passing out your business card.

Whether you turned directly from the table of contents to the Business Traveler's Checklist or have diligently read every chapter thus far, you're obviously someone who understands exactly what you need to know. You aspire to pursue international travel as though you were a counterintelligence officer, and I applaud your interest and determination. I compiled the checklist from my own experience traveling as an intelligence officer and businessman, as well as from the experiences of my seasoned consultants at SMI.

If you want to know more about who, what, where, when, why and how people engage in espionage – in particular, your competitors – then read on. You ain't seen nothin' yet!

Rock-Solid Foundation

Whenever you travel, be sure to follow the old Boy Scout motto, "Be Prepared." The level of your preparedness will often reflect the sensitivity of your business. How prepared can you get? Consider that a British technology company has recently created a memory stick that not only can be tracked via GPS but also allows the owner to send it a self-destruct command if it falls into the wrong hands. Ask yourself: *How prepared am I?*

CHAPTER 3 FAQ

9. If you regard everyone as a potential espionage operative, doesn't that tend to alienate potential clients? What's the best way to differentiate between the two?

This dilemma is nothing new; intelligence officers face it all the time. Every person they meet could be a potential recruit or a double agent who would jeopardize an operation. If the officer reveals too much too soon to a potential recruit, that officer could blow his or her cover. And if the error occurs in a hostile, Third-World country, the officer could incur imprisonment, torture or death.

The best advice whenever you encounter someone new abroad is to listen more than you talk.

Learn about the person first.

Ask more questions than you answer.

That includes what you say in your 60-second elevator pitch. Do you reveal unnecessary information that could be of value to a competitor?

At the end of each day, as you review the new contacts you've made, ask yourself these questions:

— Did any of these people say anything that sounded as if they were probing me or trying to elicit information?

— Did anyone seem too interested or eager?

— Did anyone arouse my suspicion?

— Did anything at all seem suspicious?

In such cases, trust your instincts. Recalling your daily conversations will often reveal clues you might have missed at the moment, and the process could prevent future embarrassment or harm. Most important, when you enter new contact information into your prospecting database, include short notes about the individual's personal behavior, especially if aspects concerned you. Documenting an interview is a reflective exercise and often becomes your best indicator of the presence of an operative.

10. Is there no safe way to leave a laptop or cell phone unattended, such as during an early morning run?

Not really, unless you're traveling with a trusted colleague who can mind your electronic devices while you're out. But when you're traveling alone, invest in a small or lightweight computer and a backpack. If you overlook this precaution, and you lose BI/IP or, worse, introduce a computer virus into your corporate email system, you might end up having plenty of time for jogging – in between efforts to find a new job. Incidentally, it's wise to vary the time of your run to avoid being patterned by operatives.

11. So, actions as innocent as sitting in the business lounge of an airport sending emails to a spouse could result in an operative capturing and reading them?

Absolutely!

12. What about encryption software, such as PGP? Does it provide sufficient protection?

It's useful to install Pretty Good Privacy, but encryption software only protects email in transit. If someone is surreptitiously recording your keystrokes, then encryption becomes a moot point; the operative has already obtained the content of your message.

13. When traveling to, say, Southeast Asia, what are the telltale indicators of espionage activity?

Be aware that audio and video devices could be surveilling you in your hotel room, taxi and/or meeting rooms. In virtually every city – wherever there is a dense, low-income population – bribery is rampant. Taxi drivers, maids, bellboys, secretaries and just about anyone in the service industry can be hired inexpensively to gather information about an international business traveler and sell it to espionage operatives. To some extent, these conditions hold true all over the world, but they're especially prevalent in Southeast Asia. There, just about anything can be bought and sold.

Need to know more?
Email us: questions@among-enemies.com

4. Operational Security and Your Personal Information Horizon

"There is one evil I dread, and that is, their spies."
– George Washington
on British Intelligence, March 24, 1776

Practicing OPSEC: A Case Study

Foreign intelligence efforts normally involve complementary and/ or redundant tactics. Operatives balance their plans to collect intelligence with efforts to minimize their expenditure of resources; how to get the biggest bang for their bucks – or rubles or renminbi. Counterintelligence officers learn to recognize those activities quickly and launch effective responses to thwart or eliminate potential damage. This is called operational security, or OPSEC. It's a systematic, proven process developed by the U.S. government, and it works exactly the same in business counterintelligence as well. The OPSEC process involves the following five steps:

— Identifying the critical information you must protect about your company's intentions, capabilities or activities to keep an adversary from gaining a significant advantage

— Analyzing potential threats from an adversary that could detect and exploit your vulnerabilities

— Pinpointing your company's vulnerabilities and determining how easily your adversary could acquire intelligence about them

— Determining whether your vulnerabilities might require countermeasures

— Applying appropriate countermeasures; in other words acting to negate an adversary's ability to exploit your vulnerabilities – although this is something a counterintelligence officer should never do alone or while attempting to collect intelligence.

Essentially, OPSEC provides a mindset for detecting the work of your adversaries. It charges you with eliminating – or at least minimizing – any vulnerability your adversaries could exploit to undermine your competitive position.

Protecting Your Personal Information Horizon

The term "horizon" refers to the edge of the world, as far as we can see it. It's a boundary. Your personal information horizon likewise is a boundary. It defines how much you wish to be visible to the outside world – how much of your world you want everyone else to see.

Therefore, your goal as a traveler of importance and influence in your business and industry is to confine your personal information horizon within the boundaries you have set.

Of course, it's never possible to create an impregnable personal information horizon. But you can monitor it and to some extent control what leaks out. Nor is it difficult to maintain a high level of OPSEC. It requires you to stay sharp and pay keen attention to detail and nuance.

In the intelligence community, we use two concepts to achieve this goal:

Duty of Care   This is a legal obligation. It means acting to avoid causing harm to others. One example would be to warrant that a steel girder will not fail under a specified load. The opposite, called abnegating duty of care, involves a company failing to ascertain the limits of a structural component. Or, pertinent to this book, the act would involve knowingly sending an employee into harm's way, such as to a country at war, without providing advance knowledge and preparation.

Standard of Care   Another legal obligation. It compels covered individuals to exercise an appropriate degree of caution and prudence in their personal behavior while undertaking duty-of-care responsibilities. A business traveler who consorts with felons or indulges in lascivious activities – such as the black market, drugs, prostitution and so forth – would not be exercising standard of care.

Taken together, the concepts of duty of care and standard of care underpin behavior that will place neither you nor your company's assets in harm's way. Make no mistake, this isn't as simple as saying, "Okay, I'll do it." But you don't need a law degree, either. What's required is a dedicated viewpoint about how you and your employer think about and interact with the world.

Chapter 3 presented the Business Traveler's Checklist, describing how you should regard the five major places where you're likely to be either surveilled by espionage operatives or lose your valuable BI/ IP. This chapter goes further, presenting scenarios of what can happen to a hypothetical business traveler in the airport, on a plane, in a taxi, at the hotel or at a business conference or trade show.

At the Airport   You're a partner in a commercial architectural company and are flying out of Chicago O'Hare on your way to Dubai, where you're attending a meeting to work out the final details for a new shopping mall your firm has designed. Also attending will be wealthy Arab venture-capital sheiks and princes, government officials, contractors and the mall chain's CEO with his minions. Your firm has worked on the project for over a year, and this will be the formal unveiling.

You enter the airline's VIP lounge and slip a portfolio containing your first-class ticket from your suitcoat pocket across the counter to the attractive hostess. She flashes a sweet smile and asks if she can escort you to the Premiere Club, where its fully stocked bar and hot-and-cold buffet await. As you follow her, you can't help noticing her willowy figure and graceful gait.

You order a club soda with a twist and fill a small plate with fruits, a wedge of Brie, water crackers and a dollop of Beluga caviar – too salty, you know, but you can't resist. You find a comfortable seat on a leather sofa and enjoy your snack while catching CNN Headline News on the wall-sized, flat-panel monitor.

A well-dressed man with an overcoat, hat, briefcase and carry-on plunks down beside you, finishing a call on his iPhone, which he taps off before turning to you.

"Shit, I did it again," he says, chagrined.

"What?" you ask.

"Missed my flight."

"Where are you headed?"

He lets out a big sigh.

"London. I do this a lot. Miss my flights. My boss is gonna have my ass, because he'll have to pay the change fee. I swear if I don't get my act together he'll have me paying out of my own pocket."

He eyes you for a moment.

"How about you? Where're you headed?"

"The Emirates."

"Nice! I've heard a lot about that place – the indoor skiing, the hotel suites the size of a football field, the Russian women, the desert sports car races at midnight. Good for you! First time?"

You nod.

"Business, I assume."

He digs a card out of his suit coat pocket.

"Rob Peterson," he says, sticking out his hand. "I do materials procurement for large construction projects."

"I'm in business development," you say, also mentioning you're scouting for new manufacturing facilities for your company.

"Really?" he asks. "I didn't know they manufactured in the Gulf. I thought it was just a vacation spot."

"Eh, the world is flat … or so they say."

The truth is his name isn't Rob, he did not miss his flight, and his business card is phony. The phone number is back-stopped to a voice mailbox established in a different name. His email address is a Yahoo! account. His Web site requires setting up a login and password, after which it turns into a phishing site to capture your computer's information.

Yes, Rob Peterson is a freelance espionage operative contracted by business entities. He works the various lounges at this airport, looking for targets like you: well-groomed people in fashionable business clothing, carrying an expensive briefcase, often a laptop bag – business travelers who appear familiar with the airport facilities and are accustomed to being served well.

Rob rarely selects female prey, however, because women too easily become defensive at the prospect of being approached uninvited. But his counterpart, a petite, dishwater blonde who uses the name Michelle, does the same work. She has been playing the sister-in-distress routine in the ladies' room with great success.

Rob's missed-my-flight patter is a terrific icebreaker. It gives him plenty of time to work you, to learn as much about you as he can.

Sometimes he gets brushed off by his target, usually because the prospective mark doesn't want to hear someone else's problems. Or, he's busy conducting last-minute business on his cell phone or checking email on his laptop via the airport's Wi-Fi network. In fact, Rob often hopes that's the case. He doesn't mind being snubbed, as long as he can sit nearby and try to snag information or attempt to piggy-back on your IP address and hack into your emails. Maybe you'll even get up to use the restroom and, as many travelers do, ask him to mind your belongings.

You bet he will.

If you head for the men's room, Rob will quickly slide his hand into your briefcase, feeling for your cell phone. But this is where your knowledge and training can thwart him and save you.

Instead of your phone, all Rob finds is a sealed packet of papers. He slips it out and discovers it has a taped seal he cannot interrupt without revealing his intent. He puts it back inside then turns to the laptop bag. He unzips the pockets, still looking for the phone. He only finds its battery in an outside flap. He's beginning to worry you'll be back any minute, so he quickly extracts your laptop and flips it open. He pushes the power button and produces a USB flash drive. Whoa! You have filled the USB ports with epoxy!

This guy is too savvy, he thinks.

Now he's sure you're traveling with valuable information, because you're taking such precautions.

No problem, he decides. *I'll see what's on the hard drive and use the airport Wi-Fi to upload it to my cloud.*

As soon as the computer boots up, it displays a small window that reads: ENTER YOUR PASSWORD.

"Dammit!" Rob mutters under his breath, clicking on the shutdown icon. But the computer won't shut down. He presses the power button, but the laptop remains on, the password-request window flashing away. Beginning to perspire, Rob gives up, snaps the lid closed, and bends over to put the computer back in its bag. As he does, he sees two large black shoes step in front of him. When he looks up, he's greeted by a big man with his hand resting on the butt of his side holster.

"Airport security."

Bravo! You did everything correctly. Your company's chief of security hired an ex-CIA intelligence officer, now a business travel consultant, to train you and several other colleagues. He taught you how to be on the lookout for an espionage operative, and you exercised standard of care in the way you handled this encounter. You gave Rob only a general idea of your destination. You made a generic reference to your work in buildings. And you carefully secured your personal belongings and electronics. Then, when you stood nearby, watching the operative going through your bags and confirming your initial instinctive perceptions, you called airport security, which caught him red-handed and arrested him.

On the Airplane   Don't let your guard down!

Cowboys and soldiers know this in their guts, but most business travelers don't understand the need to maintain their vigilance. You, however, acting as a counterintelligence officer-in-training, are beginning to learn this.

Airlines want you to be comfortable and relaxed as you fly, even to the point of sedating you with food, liquor, constant entertainment and blacked-out cabins. You might be further lulled into dropping your guard by the attractive – or in some instances motherly – woman sitting next to you.

What about that man in the window seat, wearing his white iPod earphones, pounding away on his laptop keyboard? Is he a threat? At least you need to be aware of him and his actions. In fact, you need to become totally aware of your personal information horizon and the people within it, especially when you're in a confined area such as an airliner or vehicle or any other space that isn't your own. Likewise, depending on your assessment of your personal or professional vulnerability, sometimes you need to keep your guard up even within your own space.

For now, let's stick with the aircraft. People often regard flying business class or first class as a luxury, but for travelers carrying sensitive BI/IP it's often a matter of taking sensible security precautions. You incur less risk when you aren't packed like a sardine in coach. There, espionage operatives could be sitting within a few feet of you at starboard, port, fore or aft.

Let's take a closer look at what a good counterintelligence officer would do to maintain personal safety and protect BI/IP on board.

You pass through TSA security and find a private spot to sit with your carry-on bag. There – if you haven't already done it – you remove your mobile phone's battery and place it in a zippered compartment in your carry-on. You fasten the zipper with a small padlock – just enough security to keep honest people honest and espionage operatives at bay. On the plane, you place your bag in the compartment directly above you. You travel with a no-frills laptop, which lacks a hard drive and therefore stores no significant data. It can only function when used in conjunction when used with a USB-delivered operating system.

You keep your flash drive containing your BI/IP in your pocket. You plug in the flash drive to work, and each time you finish you save the files on the detachable drive, which you place as close to your skin as possible.

Shortly before takeoff, the flight attendant asks if you would like a cocktail.

"No, thank you, just mineral water," you reply.

Your seatmate by the window orders two bourbons and several bags of peanuts. *He'll be fast asleep soon*, you think. In flight, you boot the computer and download a few files from the flash drive. A man in the aisle across from yours stands, stretches, and looks down at you.

"Say, that's an Ultrabook, isn't it?" he asks.

"Yes," you reply, as you close the lid.

"Mind if I ask what brand? Are you happy with it?"

You tell him you are.

He pulls a business card from his pocket and hands it to you.

"Would you mind jotting down the model number and price? I always prefer personal recommendations."

"Just set it down here on my tray," you reply, observing that it's printed with a high-gloss finish. "I'll get to it, but I'm kind of busy right now."

He nods, smiles, and returns to his seat. You brush the card underneath your computer, careful not to leave any fingerprints on it, because a fresh set of prints, collected from a high-gloss card, could possibly be used against you later in a blackmail scenario.

After dinner, you grow tired and decide to nap. You put the flash drive in your pocket and slide your computer into its slim case, where it rests on your lap, under the tray table. Sometime later, you're awakened by a touch. A male flight attendant has returned the tray table to the seat back and is attempting to take your computer bag from your knees. He can't, however, because you've put your hand through the handles, a sort of improvised handcuff.

"Sir," he says, "I thought you would be more comfortable if I put your bag in the overhead."

"I'm fine, thanks," you reply.

He walks away toward the aft end of the plane. You don't remember seeing him earlier; two female attendants were serving business class. You are well trained and wise enough never to put your electronics in the overhead bin. Preferably, you keep them under the seat in front of you, in full view. You also never place items underneath your own seat, because the person behind you could clandestinely gain access to them.

As the aircraft approaches your destination, the attendants distribute customs-declaration and immigration forms, which request personal and private information. As you discreetly fill out your forms, the man seated next to you leans over and asks if he should declare some items. If you were not filling out your forms in your portfolio, they would be clearly visible to him – your home address, passport number and more. You smile and reply that you're not sure.

At this point, it would be fair to wonder if you were being targeted by any of these individuals – even the male flight attendant – for espionage. If so, you handled each situation like a calm, confident, unobtrusive counterintelligence officer. You didn't speak to anyone unnecessarily. You drank water to avoid dehydration and intoxication. You didn't leave your fingerprints on the stranger's business card, and you protected your BI/IP.

Unfortunately, the danger doesn't end there. As a targeted

businessperson, you could be detained at customs and have your passport, computer and mobile phone taken from you, giving government agents carte blanche to learn quickly who you are, whom you work for, the nature of your business travel and everything the BI/IP stored on your devices reveals. The intelligence community calls this separation from assets.

Depending on the circumstances, you might have no choice but to surrender your bags. If so, provide the inspectors with your laptop but not the USB drive. Insist that you be allowed to stay with your items at all times. Be polite but firm when dealing with immigration and customs officials – they have the power to make your arrival a living hell.

If you think officials are overstepping their authority, demand to see their supervisor or threaten to call your embassy for assistance. Know, however, that this only works as a threat. In most cases, the embassy won't help you, even if they take your phone call.

insider tale
From Personal Experience

I was once confronted, out-of-the-blue, by a police officer in the business lounge of a busy European airport. He asked me to accompany him to a private inspection area – which was actually an airport holding cell – where he and his team rummaged through my carry-on bags. When I demanded to know what was going on, he informed me it was just a "routine check."

They discovered nothing, so they escorted me in a police car – complete with flashing lights – planeside to my awaiting Boeing 747. Two uniformed officers proceeded to walk me to my seat. I couldn't help thinking that the other passengers must have imagined me as either a VIP or a dangerous criminal in transport. In reality, the airport police wanted to send me a message: "We know who you are."

In the Taxi   Strange as it seems, taxis represents the second greatest threat to your personal information horizon. Only the hotel room is more dangerous. In a taxi, you relinquish control of your personal information horizon to the driver, the traffic, external attacks and a foreign and possibly hostile environment. If you allow the driver to put your bags in the trunk, you cede even more control. Let's see how you, as a business traveler, can enhance your safety and maintain your personal information horizon.

You exit past security, obtain local currency at the exchange booth, and head for your airline's lounge. In the restroom, you remove your suit and tie and change into a long-sleeved linen shirt, pair of tan slacks and loafers, in keeping with local dress. You don sunglasses and a cap or hat then head down the escalator to baggage claim and the departure gates. Thus disguised, you are basically unidentifiable and look as little like a traveling businessperson as possible.

At the curb you scan the row of taxis, watching travelers jump toward the next in line, allowing the driver to stow their bags in the trunk. You take note of the different cab companies and check for permits and other common identification marks. Then you look through windshields at drivers and car interiors. Finding one with which you feel the most comfortable, you wait until he is next in line then step forward. You toss your bags across the rear seat and sit close to the door, murmuring the name of a hotel. You check to assure the doors are locked and the windows up.

"Sir, welcome to Dubai," the driver says." Where have you come from?"

You ignore the question, pull a local newspaper from your pocket and begin turning pages. You see his eyes glancing at you in the rearview mirror. He wears a cell phone earpiece and microphone, and you think he might be speaking softly to someone. You're heading into the downtown area, thick with traffic. The driver puts on his left-turn signal, but you tap him on the shoulder and point straight ahead, because you've already marked the route on a map inside your magazine. He smiles, shrugs, and says "Lots of traffic." You raise the magazine and settle back into your corner, where you hope the surveillance camera cannot see you well.

The taxi stops in front of a three-star hotel. The driver points to the small video screen in the seatback, where your fare is displayed and the words INSERT CREDIT CARD are flashing. You pay the driver in local currency and get out, walking straight into the hotel.

The bellman greets you, but you wave him off and take a seat in the lobby as if waiting for someone. After reading your magazine for 10 minutes, you get up and walk to the door; you don't see your cab, but you cross the lobby and exit through a side door nonetheless. Outside, you walk a few blocks, taking several unsuspicious turns, so you can see if you're being followed. As soon as you're convinced nobody has made these various turns with you–and always look only right and left when you cross a street, never back over your shoulder– you catch another taxi outside a restaurant and resume your route to the true hotel of your destination.

Such precautions might seem excessive, but they constitute the hallmark of practical security. After all, surveillance cameras have been installed in taxis the world over to assure that the driver re- mains safe from passengers, so you have a right to feel safe as well. You also have the right to exercise extra standard of care to protect your personal information horizon.

Instead of wearing clothing that easily identifies you as an Amer- ican businessperson, you changed into everyday street dress. Your sunglasses made you difficult to identify.

Taking an extra minute or two to select a taxi and driver that appear safer to you is common sense, especially if you've ever had doubts about taxi rides in the past. What if the driver had turned left onto the side street? He might have been trying to avoid traffic, but he also could have been working with operatives waiting to intercept you. If you had sensed danger and fled the taxi, you could have taken your luggage with you, because it wasn't locked in the trunk. But the better path was to remain on the known route.

By stopping at a different hotel, you increased the chances of detecting whether you had been targeted or were being followed.

Well done – but your greatest challenge is next.

In the Hotel   As mentioned, hotels are the least-safe places for people and information alike, because guests are so vulnerable to intrusions, both personally and electronically. In many countries, hotels are owned, subsidized or controlled by the government, giv- ing espionage operatives the run of the suites. Indeed, in some cases a government will install its agents onsite to gather information and intelligence routinely.

Personal intrusions include information gathering via listening and viewing devices and by operatives going through your belongings and briefcase whenever you've left the room. Electronic intrusions involve downloading the BI/IP stored on your smartphone or computer. Here's how you can thwart them.

You check in at the front desk in the gleaming lobby of the sleek, beautiful hotel – it seems as though everything is shiny and new in Dubai – keeping a careful watch to ensure no one is standing too close to you. You see two men wearing traditional white *thawbs* talking across the lobby, but neither glances your way. That is not the case with the beautiful blonde sitting nearby. When she catches your eye, she smiles but then turns away.

A bellman accompanies you to your room on the 27th floor and, with the single key card you have requested, opens the door for you. He precedes you into the room, opening the curtains to a magnificent view of the Persian Gulf below. He lowers the temperature on the thermostat and fluffs pillows. You tip him handsomely and ask that he assure your privacy and freedom from interruptions. Yet within minutes of his exit your phone rings. It's the bellman, asking if a woman may bring welcoming gifts to your room.

"No," you reply. "Ask her to wait in the lobby by the waterfall, and I'll come down to meet her."

You intentionally delay your appearance for 15 minutes, during which time you once again remove your cell phone battery from your carry-on, zip up the bag, and set it precisely on your bed. You take your identification, important papers, laptop and phone with you. When you enter the lobby, the woman is nowhere to be seen.

When you return to your floor, you see your door is open a crack. Entering, you find the housekeeper has changed your linens and towels. Odd, because you've just arrived and haven't even washed your face. Your carry-on has, of course, been moved to the luggage stand in the closet, and your briefcase is now lying on the Louis XIV desk; you will not be able to determine if either has been opened.

You smile at the housekeeper, tip her, and ask her to leave so you may get some rest.

Lying on your bed, you discreetly scan the room for a video camera or places where microphones or cameras might be hidden. As I keep stressing, be careful doing this. Don't be obvious or do a walk-through inspection of your room. You should also know by now that if intelligence people spot you searching for hidden devices, they could make the rest of your visit most uncomfortable.

The desk is set near the center of the room, obviously so it can be surveilled. You mentally select another location where you can work with your back against a bare wall.

You get up and unpack your carry-on, slowly putting clothing items in the dresser and carrying your Dopp kit into the bathroom. There, you spill some of your toiletries onto the floor. While kneeling down to pick things up, you quickly scan for cameras or microphones. This might seem paranoid, but any time you must examine an area of your room, make sure you've created a plausible cover for doing so.

insider tale
Water Closeting

It became common during the Cold War for spies to confer with assets in their hotel bathroom while filling the tub or flushing the toilet to disguise their conversations. The practice died out with the advent of video surveillance capabilities.

Now out of the bathroom, you turn the television on and point the remote at the screen, slowly changing channels as you pace back and forth in front of the bed. In your hand, underneath the remote, is a bug-detection gadget that emits a soft vibration when it senses a surveillance device. It finds three, and their location confirms your plan to move the desk. Otherwise, you are the picture of nonchalance.

To Scan or Not to Scan

You might be thinking, "Does he seriously want me to scan my room surreptitiously for hidden surveillance devices?"

My answer is, "It depends."

If you're a lone business traveler in a country with a hostile intelligence service, one which could arrest you for any suspicious activity, then by all means avoid doing anything suspicious. It would be difficult for you to explain why you're carrying an RF detector, for example.

On the other hand, if you and your team are negotiating a business deal worth mega-millions, you might want to avoid the need to scan your room personally by bringing along a security expert equipped with top-flight but innocuous technical gear – but recognize that even the best technical surveillance countermeasures, or TSCM, cannot detect all devices with 100-percent certainty.

In either case, avoid any confidential discussions in your room or any other location that could be surveilled by audio and/ or video.

You will be staying two days and nights, and in less than an hour you have performed a thorough assessment of the threats and vulnerabilities present in your lodging. This is a five-star hotel; although other guests do not appear to pose a threat, you feel concerned about the staff. You have found surveillance bugs in the room, but you cannot know whether they are always active or intended specifically for you. No matter; you know the scope of your personal information horizon and have determined how best to exercise your standard of care.

Whenever you leave the hotel room, you take your BI/IP and electronic devices with you. Your USB flash drive must remain on your person. Whenever you work in the room, you must sit with your back against that blank wall.

When you finish your work, you put everything back in your briefcase and close it. You don't use your mobile phone in the room, and you keep the battery in your pants pocket. If you need to make a business call, you don't use the room phone but instead go

outdoors to call from your disposable mobile, which is free of unnecessary contact numbers.

At the Meeting   You leave the room to have dinner, accompanied by your identification, briefcase, papers, laptop and phone. You
also take them along on a leisurely stroll around this beautiful city
– in part to have a look at the site of your future mall.

When you return, you have a message at the front desk. The male
clerk has been replaced by a beautiful Arab woman with thick black
hair flowing down to her waist. She hands you a small envelope
with your name emblazoned in elegant gold calligraphy. She smiles
and welcomes you again to Dubai, asking if your visit is for business
or pleasure. You secretly wish it were pleasure but politely evade the
question, thank her, and retire to your room.

You carefully study the envelope to determine if it has been un-
sealed and feel assured it is intact. Inside is a note from the CEO
of the mall-development company, informing you that a limousine
will arrive in the morning to take you to the meeting. You will be
identified by the code word provided.

You click the television remote to one of the OSN channels and
fall asleep watching a rerun of a ridiculous action movie from the
late '80s. You chuckle to yourself about how popular they still seem
to be in the Middle East.

Next morning, at 9:30, six stretch Mercedes limos sit in the hotel
turnaround. Six Arab men in black suits, white shirts, black ties and
keffiyehs stand alongside, each holding a sign. You approach and scan
the names, one of which is your code word. You tell the driver your
name; he nods and opens the limo's door.

The meeting begins and proceeds smoothly. You are surprised at
how well everyone gets along with one another, as if they all were
aware that cooperation ensured a successful working relationship. A
cocktail party ends the meeting. Several of the men engage you in
conversation, which continues through a long and pleasant dinner.

The limo returns you to your hotel, where the same beautiful
clerk is on duty. You've had a few glasses of wine and an aperitif,
which have loosened your inhibitions a bit, and you begin chatting.

You are tempted to boast about your new project and its imminent success, but your wits take over and you remember your standard of care. You confine your conversation to small talk and eventually take leave of her.

The second day of meetings is as successful as the first. In the morning your client approves your plans, and all that remains is for the home office to transmit the contract for signatures. This is accomplished after lunch, and you tuck the signed documents into your briefcase to carry home the next morning. Your chauffeur drives you back to your hotel, and as you cross the lobby you once again encounter the lovely desk clerk. She has just finished the afternoon shift and in a low but flirtatious voice asks you to dinner. You're taken aback by the offer, because Middle Eastern women typically never act this forward in public. Before you answer, she warns you must meet discreetly; she is forbidden to associate with guests.

What do you do? First, ask yourself why a woman who knows nothing about you in a sea of eligible men would choose you because of a casual conversation the day before. The answer will guide you to tell her, politely, "Thanks, but no thanks." But maybe you decide to ask her why she seems interested in you.

She replies, "I find you very nice and very handsome."

Now you know you're being set up. Was there any way she might have known you were carrying signed contracts for a large-scale development project? It's pointless to speculate. For now, get out of harm's way. Nothing good can result from further interaction.

You excuse yourself from the temptation of her eyes, her smile, her golden-brown skin and get yourself to your room. Twelve hours later, you are on the flight home. Your ego has enjoyed a boost, even if it was only a setup for blackmail, but that's a harmless fantasy. Mission accomplished with maximum OPSEC. You made good decisions, and your firm's security officer did an excellent duty-of-care job training you and instilling standard of care.

You've become a pro. You're now a counterintelligence officer in the private sector.

CHAPTER 4 FAQ

14. If you don't drink, are you less vulnerable to being targeted?
Even if you don't consume alcohol at all, the threat from someone slipping a narcotic into your beverage still exists. For example, in Rio de Janeiro, the scam of covertly sprinkling a drug into a stranger's glass is known as Good Night Cinderella. Numerous tourists fall victim to this each year and are subsequently robbed and sometimes harmed.

Always watch your drink being made, and always ask the waitress to open bottles at your table.

15. Everyone talks about China as the biggest offender of economic and industrial espionage. What is their official response to the accusations?
The Chinese government insists they do not conduct economic or industrial espionage. Yet they refuse to recognize the U.S. Economic Espionage Act of 1996. What does that tell you?

16. What would be wrong with having a little fun with a marked operative and making up false information about yourself or your company?
That might seem like an appropriate eye-for-an-eye response, but if the operative recognizes that you've been purposely lying, the danger could escalate for you. Don't play with fire. If you think you're being elicited, your best bet is to act dumb and change the topic of conversation – but report the encounter to appropriate security personnel.

17. What's the best way to respond to blackmail attempts?
In every documented case where blackmail has occurred, the longer the victim waited to come forward, the worse the situation became. Providing secrets to a blackmailer relinquishes control of your life. If you've been targeted, consider retaining a good and trusted lawyer – outside of your corporate pool of lawyers.

18. What's the going rate for selling secrets to competitors?
Every industry is different. Sometimes instead of cash the reward comprises perks such as insider-trading information, electronics, tickets to sporting events or all-expense-paid vacations and gift cards. The typical secrets-for-cash transaction involving high-value BI/IP runs minimum US$50,000.

Need to know more?
Email us: questions@among-enemies.com

5. Cyber-Espionage

"We are losing data, we are losing money, we are losing ideas and we are losing innovation. Together we must find a way to stop the bleeding."

– FBI Director Robert S. Mueller III, speaking before the RSA Conference in San Francisco in March 2012, where he expressed the view that cyber-threats would surpass terrorism as the country's top concern[15]

How to Protect Your Electronic Devices

Cyber-espionage poses the greatest threat to the business traveler, because it is so easy to perpetrate. It has replaced many of the old, tried-and-true methods such as human surveillance; stealing your briefcase or documents; or breaking into your hotel room, copying your documents, and even taking tiny photographs with a spy camera.

Now, surveillance can be accomplished using GPS tracking via your smartphone or your vehicle's onboard computer. Stealing or borrowing paper documents has been replaced by sophisticated operations sharply targeted at businesspeople, such as keystroke logging and other techniques to extract BI/IP from their electronic devices, often remotely.

The Internet, and in particular Wi-Fi networks, make it possible to access any kind of file, far exceeding the ability of snapping micro-photographs. It is possible to steal BI/IP by disabling encryption, breaching firewalls or other type of authentication, using any number of networking technologies without your knowledge and with little if any risk of exposure on the part of the espionage operative.

These are the risks and realities of the new competitive world, and you ignore them at your peril and that of your company.

Most Americans have heard or seen news stories for years about criminals hacking into corporate computer systems to steal credit-card information, plant malware and viruses, read email and confidential documents or create false identities – but not stories about thefts of proprietary business information. The counterintelligence officer/business traveler must be ever alert to the dangers posed by cyber-espionage. More important, it's a moving target; the technological advances come rapidly and furiously. This chapter gives a general overview of the various technologies and the tactics, techniques and procedures – TTP, in the parlance of intelligence officers – used to exploit information systems and covertly exfiltrate, or steal, BI/IP.

Basic Cyber-Espionage Rules to Follow While Traveling

By this point, you should be well aware that **Rule 1**, introduced in Chapter 1, represents an essential guidepost for you.

— Assume you are under surveillance by someone who wants your BI/IP.

— Never assume you're too insignificant to be targeted, so learn to think and act like a counterintelligence officer.

Rule 1 and its corollary apply whenever and wherever you travel, whether in your car or a limo from home to office, on an Amtrak train between cities or on an international flight. Regardless of where you travel or how, you need to remember that rule, plus a few more variations:

— Assume any wireless connection is compromised and capable of exposing your electronic device to virtual theft.

— Back up your electronic devices to the corporate server, the cloud, and again to a local device, at least twice a week and always before departing on a business trip.

— Change your passwords frequently. Make them at least eight characters long and include a variety of uppercase and lowercase letters, numbers and special characters. Passphrases are the easiest to remember, but store them in an encrypted or password-protected file that *does not* reside on your computer or smartphone.

— Never plug in a USB flash drive given to you as a gift or promotional swag. Turn them over to your security office for analysis.

— Never let electronic devices out of your personal possession or sight for any reason.

— Employ full disk encryption on all laptops when traveling. Use encrypted, removable storage devices.

— Use designated travel laptops and phones. Have IT personnel create key files using the hash function.

— Don't make your password recovery hint question too easy. For example, for "What is your mother's maiden name?" don't use the real one. Instead, use someone from your past that no one else would know.

— Take brand-new SD cards and USB drives when you travel. Even if you've deleted a file from one of these devices, clever operatives and intelligence services can use off-the-shelf technology to recover it.

— Turn off the GPS location and metadata features on your phone before you travel to thwart attempts to triangulate your location and movement via cell towers. Likewise, disable the GPS location feature on your phone's camera photos.

— Another reason to use a disposable cell phone: Even if you've swapped out your regular phone's SIM card, the phone's root memory still contains its ID number, which can be used to identify you.

Which Electronic Devices and Services Place You at Risk?

For business travelers, preparing and packing electronic devices has become as important as suits and ties. You need to bring critical business documents, as files on your computer as well as on paper, to your meetings. You might need to work on a speech, a PowerPoint presentation or a business plan, and you might want to take along the latest Lee Child thriller on your ebook reader to pass your idle moments. Perhaps you'll want to listen to a recorded book or some music on your iPod or iPad. You might be thinking about some last-minute research you want to conduct online using the in-flight Wi-Fi service.

On top of all this, different tasks still require different devices, so business travelers commonly carry an array of them: a laptop or tablet computer; a mobile phone or smartphone; one or more USB flash drives; an iPod, iPad or other portable listening/viewing device – such as an Android, Nook or Kindle – and, commonly, a pair of Bose noise-canceling headphones, which, thankfully, pose no cyber-threat, plus a digital still and/or video camera.

What you store on any of these devices can be of potential interest to espionage operatives. Furthermore, business travelers place themselves at high risk when they use the following services while on the road:

— Wi-Fi networks in the airport, on the aircraft, in the hotel or in public venues such as coffee shops

— Social media Web sites or services such as Facebook, Twitter or LinkedIn

— Email

— Business data file transfers, either between devices such as a flash drive and computer or by accessing corporate or cloud servers from remote or unsecured locations

— Business or personal calls from any phone, whether in the hotel room or via cell

— Uploading and downloading images, videos, apps and other miscellany

Electronic devices such as tablets or cameras that use memory cards, which can be accessed and have malware installed, also are vulnerable.

insider tip
Traveling with Smartphones

If you must carry a smartphone when you travel, beware of downloading apps or wallpaper. Even the most popular apps can be spoofed, thereby infecting your phone with spyware. Just because you bought an app from the iTunes store doesn't mean it's 100-percent safe.

Also, be sure to turn off all GPS locating devices and pay attention to both the battery drain and monthly expenses on your phone. If your battery seems to deplete itself more quickly than expected, or if your monthly charges have increased inexplicably, your device might be harboring malware.

How can you curb the threat of cyber-espionage? Can you simplify the task of protecting your electronic devices and the data they store, thereby reducing your cyber-theft exposure? To start, you don't need to take along as many devices or as much data as you think, and the less you take the more you reduce your risk of compromising or losing BI/IP.

Following the model we established in Chapter 3 and Chapter 4, we'll use the Business Traveler's Checklist – plus an extra category – to illustrate the proper ways to carry and handle your electronic devices and the information and the intelligence they contain.

At the Airport   We probably should have titled this section "Anywhere between Your Home and Office and the Airport," because make no mistake, anyone traveling in a suit, or with a briefcase and computer bag, attracts the attention of espionage operatives. Moreover, if you work in one of the targeted industries – typically science and technology – you must assume that someone is surveilling you the day of your departure. Operatives want to know who you are and what you do, so they watch your house and your office, and they watch where you come and go.

Don't doubt this. Every day in the legal world, multi-million-dollar lawsuits are settled out of court, protected by secrecy agreements, or they are brought to trial in public and often embarrassing courtroom battles. In many instances, the decision to fight publicly or quietly settle hinges on a single piece of insider intelligence. For example, if the lead defense counsel for a major pharmaceutical firm walks out of his house with a suitcase and gets into a taxi, the plaintiff's operatives, who have been watching him, will assume he's leaving on a trip that could affect the case, so they will follow him. Even if he drives his car to work, they'll attempt to determine if he's got luggage in his trunk.

Sound like a John Grisham novel? Perhaps, but when large sums or trade secrets are involved you can fairly assume someone is being surveilled.

Therefore, you need a plan to protect your BI/IP – including what your electronic devices are holding.

HARDWARE   Prepare your computer and phone for travel

before you leave home or the office – whichever is your site of departure. Better yet, maintain a separate computer that you use only for traveling; one that can be wiped clean of data or have its hard drive removed and replaced after each trip.

BACKUP   Back up your entire computer, including data, applications, everything – twice – once on your corporate server and/or the secure cloud and again on a local device such as your desktop computer or a portable flash drive you can secure. It's reasonable to assume that operatives can gain access to your office, for example, posing as a member of the cleaning crew.

Consequently, don't forget to wipe your whiteboards clean, lock up your Rolodex and appointment book, and remove important sticky notes from your monitor.

Next, delete everything you won't need for your trip, including your browser history, email program and instant messages, as well as your address book.

EMAIL   As mentioned in Chapter 3, when you travel, either use an alias on a disposable account from a free service or install a secure email program. On that score you have several options, such as a Web-based service with Pretty Good Privacy (PGP) encryption or a domain-based email server that provides near-total isolation and security.

In other words, for secure communications, invest in an email address that resides on a private server. Then give that address only to those with whom you plan to correspond while traveling. You can delete the account when your travel ends and open a new one for your next trip.

APPS AND DATA   Store only what you expect to use on the trip. Uninstall your normal Web browser and install a different one – preferably with a new user name and password – to ensure that your former browser history, bookmarks, cached pages, cookies and stored passwords do not accompany you. Avoid using Web sites that require a login and password, particularly banking or financial sites. So, pay your monthly bills in advance before leaving, in case your trip is extended unexpectedly, and don't buy anything online while traveling. If you have not done so, install an encryption program on your hard drive and a login and password for power-up access to the computer.

POWER DOWN   Log out and switch off the power on all electronic devices before you leave home or the office. Disable the Wi-Fi function and/or remove the battery from your phone and computer. Pack them and other electronic devices in innocuous-looking or unconventionally designed bags such as a backpack or messenger bag; for example, something sold by luggage maker Tom Bihn.

It's also a good idea to power down your mobile phone each week to allow the manufacturer to transmit updated anti-virus software during the restart.

PASSWORDS   The best place to store user names and passwords is in your head, if you can remember them. For travel, use an unidentifiable gibberish name that cannot be associated with you and a long, maximum-strength password. Create a mnemonic to remember your user name and password to avoid writing them down, or store them in an encrypted file on your flash drive. If you can't do either, write them somewhere discreet, such as in the margins of the novel you're reading. Use arcane and impersonal logins and passwords, and don't use the same ones for everything.

> **insider tip**
> **Protect Your Voicemail**
> Cell phones can be easily spoofed, allowing espionage operatives to listen to your voicemail messages. All it takes is your phone number. Using an inexpensive online service, the caller spoofs, or pretends to be calling from your own number to your number. Then all the operative has to do is punch the * or # key to listen. How can you prevent this? Set up a password or PIN that must be entered before anyone can listen to voicemail.

If you need assistance with any of these preparations, talk to your corporate IT or security people. They'll likely have recommended and approved software available to install.

When you reach the airport, promptly clear security and check in at your gate. Wandering around the shops or having a meal outside the secured area is a sure way to expose yourself to operatives. Never leave your personal belongings unattended, even for a moment and particularly not in the care of a stranger sitting next to you – no matter how trustworthy he or she looks. **Rule 1. Rule 1. Rule 1.** At all times, assume you're being surveilled. In fact, you *are* being constantly surveilled by airport security, but we're talking about intelligence operatives, who are more surreptitious. Change seats or get up frequently in the airport lounge or at the gate. Watch for individuals who move with you.

> **insider tale**
> **Hacking an International Airport**
> In August, 2012, a vast hacker attack at a foreign airport (which remains unidentified for security purposes) was discovered by an American security company. With a single click to open a Web site, operatives downloaded a type of malware dubbed Man in the Browser, or MiB, and installed it on the airport's computer system. It allowed intruders to read the screens of employees logged in remotely to the airport's VPN, granting them access to the entire system. [16]
>
> Experts suspect their intent was to penetrate the airport's financial records, but the intruders also could have gained access to air-traffic control and even such systems as the air conditioning. In addition, MiB captured the logins and passwords of all business travelers using the airport's Wi-Fi network.

You can obtain some protection, but not complete assurance, by using Web browser software features such as Internet Explorer's In-Private Browsing option, which deletes the history of Web sites you visited and any accompanying cookies. This does not protect you against files intentionally or unintentionally downloaded, however, so don't use public or purportedly free Wi-Fi hotspots anywhere.

Ever. Period.

On the Plane   It's probably unrealistic for you to avoid using your laptop or tablet aboard the aircraft; after all, you want to take advantage of a quiet time to get things done or simply relax with a book or a movie.

Fair enough, but assess your environment before using your electronic devices. Are you seated in business class or first class? That means you have only one seatmate and perhaps the passenger across the aisle to assess. If you travel in economy or coach, your risk is greater, because you're potentially in much closer observational and electronic proximity to an operative.

Your personal information horizon is considerably more difficult to maintain in coach, because more people have access to the overhead compartments, and there is no rule requiring passengers to stow their bags directly above their own row. Watch for individuals who open the compartment above you who are seated elsewhere in the aircraft; they could be looking for poorly-attended BI/IP goodies.

ACCESS VIA CONTACT   A less-complex way for an espionage operative to get at your BI/IP is by physically stealing or accessing your electronic devices, in particular those sitting in the overhead compartment. A smart operative will note what you've stowed then root through your belongings while you're napping or in the lavatory.

You should never voluntarily store anything sensitive away from your personal information horizon, but sometimes you have no choice. If that's the case, make sure your computer password is activated. Remove the battery from your phone, if you haven't already done so, and put it in your pocket. Although you cannot lock your bags when passing through security, you can certainly lock them before they go in the overhead.

The best option is to stow your devices in your bag and tuck it between your feet, or hold it on your lap, so you are in constant physical contact.

ACCESS WITHOUT CONTACT   Your BI/IP could be at risk even if the operative has not made physical contact with your electronic devices. Devices that feature IR ports or Bluetooth links can give up their data if the operative can position his or her computer close enough. It's a slow connection, but given enough time – such as on an international flight – the IR port can easily be used to siphon data from your computer or implant malware.

To counter this prospect, first locate your port. It's a red plastic rectangle on the computer's left or right side. Is the individual in the seat next to you or across the aisle using a computer? Is your computer's IR port exposed? If so, take evasive action. Ideally, disable it using the operating system command. But an effective quick fix is to cover the port with your hand or, perhaps, set a book in front of it.

By the way, many cell phones have IR ports as well – though not the iPhone.

Bluetooth wireless connections are ubiquitous on cell phones and computers. Their most common use for phones is to connect a headset; for computers they link to the mouse and keyboard. The Bluetooth signal is stronger than IR – enough, for example, to connect your wireless headset to your phone. This capability makes them more vulnerable to hacking. In fact, hacking Bluetooth connections has become so popular that some Web sites now offer hackers the requisite software. One even sports the title "7 Most Popular Bluetooth Hacking Software To Hack Mobile Phones."

The two most effective ways to block an attempted Bluetooth hacker are 1) disable the Bluetooth port, and 2) create a unique password. Most people never change it from the factory setting, which is commonly 0000. Learn how to disable the port on your phone and computer. Again, this involves corporate security, so if you need help, ask your people.

SCREEN DISCRETION   Another concern is whether your seatmate, or the potential operative sitting in the row behind you, can spy what's on your screen. Even people walking the aisle can see what you're doing. Unless you're playing solitaire, it's wise to disguise your activities, especially if you're working on a business document.

To thwart possible surveillance, adjust the screen's brightness to the lowest level you can tolerate. If you have a privacy filter, by all means use it. However you do it, keep those sitting beside or near you from being able to read what's on your screen.

USING YOUR PHONE   Unless that last-minute call is absolutely crucial, avoid phoning while aboard the aircraft. It's important to refrain from using your phone unnecessarily while traveling, not only because it's simple good manners but also to eliminate the chance of you blurting out something an operative would love to hear. Sometimes, travelers will turn their smartphones on but not make calls while in flight. Then they'll write emails to send later or play games or just check the time. But anytime that phone is on, it becomes susceptible to intrusion or hacking.

Always lock your phone with either a PIN or password phrase. You never know when you might accidentally leave it behind somewhere.

USING WI-FI   Wireless Internet connections have become more prevalent on airliners, but that doesn't mean you should use them. Airborne Wi-Fi is notoriously insecure on two counts. First, in-flight Internet does not offer encryption; therefore it is no more trusted than the Wi-Fi hotspot at your favorite coffee shop. Second, unless you delete the in-flight Internet service from your computer, it will continue searching for a connection after you deplane.

Here's the problem: If you want to know how many Wi-Fi connections are active on your computer, you've got to look for them. You could easily forget that the airline's wireless service is still available. But if you fail to delete that network, you could be spoofed by an operative using an IP address purporting to be the in-flight service.

The spoof is simple. Your computer's Wi-Fi receiver is still searching for the host carrier signal. If it interprets an incoming signal as the in-flight service, it will accept it, rendering you vulnerable and exposed.

If you must use Wi-Fi when traveling, do so over a VPN, which encrypts Internet transmissions so no one except the communicating devices can understand or interpret the data stream. VPNs are commonly used as corporate-wide services, but private networks offer paid access for individuals who wish to visit Web sites and send email more securely.

insider tale
Emulating the French
In 2000, the People's Republic of China purchased a 767 jetliner from the Boeing Corporation for their Communist leader Jiang Zemin to use as China's version of the U.S. President's Air Force One aircraft. When the plane arrived in Beijing, however, Chinese security officials discovered 27 sophisticated electronic eavesdropping devices in the aircraft. [17]

In the Taxi   Taxi drivers typically fall into the category of free-lance private collectors. It makes sense. Who's in a better position to scan arriving business travelers and determine if they are ripe for espionage? Some are highly skilled, having been recruited and trained by government intelligence officers or corporate agents, or both. Every conceivable type of surveillance device can be hidden inside a cab, making it a cyber snake pit for your electronic devices.

The probing isn't confined to electronics. Many business travelers chat openly with taxi drivers, often because they're excited to be in a new city or country, or simply to abate the silence of a long ride. If the driver speaks your language, all the better; perhaps you can get some tips on where to go at night or shop for gifts.

Sure, there's little harm in striking up a simple conversation about your visit, although the hotel concierge or brochures left in your room should tell you all you want to know. But if you want to be chatty, make sure you're also wary of being asked too many personal questions. Under no circumstances reveal to the taxi driver the nature of your travel, your occupation, with whom you're meeting, how long you're staying, or anything about where you live or your family members.

Is the taxi bugged? It's unlikely you will be able to detect surveillance devices in the taxi, but assume they're there, from a camera pointed at you from the TV mounted in the driver's seatback to microphones hidden in the headliner or in the fobs dangling from the ceiling – even in the stuffed animal sitting on the rear window shelf. Bear in mind that surveillance equipment protects the taxi driver from criminals, too, so its primary purpose might not be espionage.

For example, four intoxicated women once accused a Canadian taxi driver of sexual assault, but his camcorder recording proved nothing had happened. The women were using the ploy to evade paying cab fare.

In any event, if you're traveling with a business companion, don't discuss anything relating to your work or the trip. Keep your cell phone turned off and the battery removed.

In some countries, such as the United Kingdom, taxis are

required by law to carry surveillance equipment as a crime deterrent. Legal issues aside, the wisest course of action might be to watch the progress to your destination in silence. Pay the driver in cash – not by credit card. And never call attention to a surveillance device if you happen to see one. In fact, never indicate you think you are under surveillance.

Put another way, mum's the word. Act like the most uninteresting person on the planet.

Incidentally, this same rule applies to rental vehicles, because it's easy for operatives to place listening devices inside them. Indeed, most already carry unencrypted audio systems for calling roadside assistance. Be careful not to conduct business in a rental vehicle – you never know who might be listening.

In the Hotel   As mentioned earlier, the hotel is the riskiest place for the business traveler. It possesses all the various means of compromising you and gaining access to your BI/IP, as described in Chapter 2: blackmail, bribery, eavesdropping, electronic surveillance and interception, elicitation, intrusion, misdirection and possibly even physical attack. You are exceedingly vulnerable in a hotel; you're not on home turf, and it's difficult to discern the good guys from the bad. Therefore, exercise extreme caution in all your actions, and assume that anyone you meet, staff or guest alike, could be an operative or someone working with one.

insider tale
The New Breeding Ground for Espionage
A colleague of mine was staying in a New York garden hotel recently. After breakfast, he decided to hop on Google Maps to check the distance to his first appointment, seeing if it was close enough to walk. The concierge told him where to find the house computer room, located off the main lobby.

"You'll need your room key to enter. Security, you know."

There, he observed five computers, all in use, with everyone on Facebook, reading and writing messages.

"Gathering intelligence from social media finally has become as 'sexy' as more traditional clandestine methods," reports Esther Carey on Federal News Radio.

"Open-source intelligence, generally regarded as information gathered through methods other than clandestine activity, is the 'hot new field' in the intelligence community," remarked Patrick O'Neil, director of analytic development at the Open Source Center in the Office of the Director of National Intelligence. Intelligence agencies are developing their capabilities to gather useful information by scouring social media platforms such as Twitter and Facebook.

Obviously, operatives could have had a field day with the quintet at the hotel.

Espionage often occurs within the chain of events listed above, as you observed in the story told in the Introduction. You, as a practitioner of counter-espionage, must be alert at all times when you travel.

For example, does the cabbie run up to converse with the doorman or concierge as soon as you arrive at your hotel?

Does the desk captain or the bellhop ask to take your luggage and your briefcase or computer bag?

Does the hotel offer you a "special" suite?

Does the hotel deliver flowers or fruit, or does the staff offer you complimentary use of the spa or exercise room after you first enter your room?

Does the maid or housekeeper knock on your door at an unexpected hour to ask if you need more towels or to check the mini-bar?

These are all red flags to alert you that surveillance or espionage could be under way.

STAYING SAFE IN YOUR HOTEL ROOM   First, assume there are audio, and possibly video, devices monitoring your communications. Therefore, don't use the phone – cell or house – or meet with colleagues in your room. In fact, don't even talk to yourself, because it's possible to activate the microphone in your cell phone remotely and record every utterance – one more good reason to keep the battery removed.

If you must use your computer, say, to write reports or examine documents, disable its Wi-Fi connectivity. Don't hook up to an Ethernet cable, either. If there's an Ethernet router on the desktop, make sure it's turned off but don't unplug it, because it will arouse suspicion. Don't sit at the desk to work; a hidden camera could be trained over your shoulder. Speaking of which, hidden cameras are commonly concealed in smoke detectors and light fixtures. Likewise, if the room's mirrors are bolted to the wall, you can at least assume there's a camera operating behind the glass.

insider tip
Mirror Tests Aren't So Simple
Urban legend has it that if you hold your fingernail against a mirror's surface, and you can't see a gap between the nail and its reflection, then it could be two-way, and you could be under surveillance.

   Two problems: 1) Even a conventional mirror can be compromised by clever operatives using, say, a tiny hole in the wall behind the mirror and a miniature camera with a wide-angle lens. 2) If you are under surveillance and you perform the fingernail trick, or do anything else suspicious, you'll immediately heighten interest in your activities.

GOING ONLINE   If you must connect to the Internet, watch out for an unencrypted Wi-Fi signal on the dropdown list of local network providers. Operatives will often check into hotels during large conventions and broadcast their own free Wi-Fi, usually with a strong connection. Then they watch for guests who forgo the paid hotel Internet service in favor of their free alternative. If someone takes the bait, they can monitor that person's online activity.

Also, don't set up your computer using your true name, such as "Luke's MacBook" or "SMI-PC1." Instead, use random numbers and letters that can't identify you on the Wi-Fi network, whatever its source.

WASTE NOT   Don't use the shredder or copier provided in your room. Either one could actually be remotely scanning your documents. When in doubt, tear up scraps of paper containing notes or telephone numbers into tiny pieces and flush them down your bathroom toilet. Or, soak your papers in the bathtub, crumple them up into balls of mush, and then dump them in the trash.

Why go to so much trouble? Because chambermaids and operatives routinely search hotel-room wastebaskets.

Once again, never actively look for an audio or video device in your hotel room. Sure, James Bond did it in *Dr. No* and *From Russia with Love*, but he was adept at eliminating anyone who might confront him. If you try it, you might mistakenly persuade your watchers you're a spy. Don't make it easy for an espionage team or intelligence service to decide to keep tabs on you.

If you can, work on your computer or make your calls outdoors or at least away from your hotel room. And when you watch movies in your room on your iPad or tablet, remember that those devices can be accessed by hackers, so never leave them unattended and make sure they aren't storing anything sensitive.

Also, if you're carrying a tablet as well as a laptop – which means you've got two devices to protect instead of one – don't connect to the Internet with both of them.

insider tale
Life Imitates Art

Speaking of hidden cameras and *Dr. No*, I once checked into a hotel room in Taipei, Taiwan. Sitting on the bed, I switched the television on and, in a bit of irony, tuned in just in time to see the original James Bond movie, dubbed in Chinese. I noticed a flicker of light or a reflection of some kind just beneath the TV screen.

It was a tiny video camera.

Shocked that it was pointed at the bed – no doubt to capture inappropriate activity that could later be used for blackmail – I called down to the front desk to complain. At first, the manager attempted to persuade me what I had seen under my television was not a camera, but after I sternly insisted I knew what a camera looked like, he apologized and explained that I was staying in a "special room" and that the camera was there to monitor elderly and disabled guests who required possible assistance. He then assured me the camera was not operating.

Just as 007 did, I requested a new room.

Which brings up a good point: You might want to get into the habit of always switching rooms after you check in. Accept the original room, but on initial inspection request a different room. You can claim that the mattress is too hard, you don't like the view, the room smells smoky, and so forth.

I've heard intelligence professionals complain about having a room fully prepared with surveillance equipment, only to have the target abruptly switch rooms at the last minute, thereby blowing the operation. In some hotels, only one room might be surveillance capable. You can improve your odds of avoiding surveillance if you get in the habit of changing rooms.

At the Meeting   I'm basing this section on the premise that your company has properly vetted the company with which you are meeting, at least to the extent both parties have established economic détente. It doesn't mean you completely trust them, however. With that in mind, consider entering their building and offices with the same standard of care you would exercise in any other unfamiliar or public venue.

It has become common for the greeter or receptionist to ask visitors to relinquish their mobile phones when entering a business's premises. If they ask this of you, don't resist. But do one of two things:

— Power down and remove the phone's battery, stowing it in your pocket.

— Power down and place the phone inside an anti-static or cloaking bag, which effectively blocks RF transmission and reception.

Neither option will prevent a truly nefarious company from opening your cloaking bag, powering up your phone, connecting it to a computer, and downloading its contents. To prevent this, you would need to lock the bag. Once again, the simplest solution is to carry a disposable phone and delete anything compromising before you go to the meeting.

The same holds true for your computer.

The best way to avoid having sensitive intelligence stolen is to leave it at home. Take only those documents or files you feel completely at ease sharing with your business partner.

Assume the company has installed surveillance cameras and microphones in elevators, restrooms, hallways, the reception area and conference rooms. Say nothing you would rather your business host did not hear.

insider tale
Business Etiquette with a Purpose
In Japan, it is customary to ask guests who have arrived for a business meeting to wait in a reception area. While the receptionist fetches them a welcoming cup of tea, the guests are left temporarily unattended. It is widely rumored that many waiting areas are wired for audio, the aim of which is to catch businesspeople discussing their strategy before entering an important meeting. Such information can provide a small but important advantage to the host. The waiting-room conversation might reveal a tip to assist in a later negotiations or an insight into the guests' mindset.

Business gatherings, whether trade shows or professional conferences, can offer a virtual smorgasbord of intelligence opportunities for espionage operatives. Businesspeople tend to show off at such gatherings with sharp dress, expensive briefcases or bags and ultra-cool electronics. You might see a man standing with his face buried in a MacBook Air or a woman talking on a 24-carat gold iPhone. But the message they are sending to operatives is, "Hey! Look at me! I'm a great target!"

As I've explained, intelligence officers are taught to look and act as inconspicuous as possible. By reading and studying this book, you are becoming a counterintelligence officer in the war against espionage, so the advice applies to you as well.

Carry your valuable electronic devices in a less-than-obvious bag.

As much as possible, mind your own business at lectures or briefings, and keep your own counsel. For example, if you have a question for a speaker during a lecture, don't stand up during the Q&A and identify yourself in front of the audience and share what's on your mind. Doing so reveals too much about yourself and your thinking.

A better tack is to approach the speaker privately afterward. The big mouths – people who interrupt speakers just to hear themselves talk or try to impress others – make tempting targets for operatives.

We'll get into the potential pratfalls of ego later.

More Hazards Online   Many conference halls are now equipped with Wi-Fi, making you a sitting duck if you log on.

Refrain from using your phone or taking notes on your laptop. Use paper and pen instead.

On the trade-show floor, keep your phone and computer switched off.

Never accept a flash drive from a vendor or any other stranger. Inserted into your computer's USB port, it can instantly and automatically install malware or keystroke-capturing software. This also reinforces the wisdom of using a laptop specifically for travel, but bear in mind you also don't want to log on to that laptop when you return home without first either performing a low-level reformatting of the hard drive or removing and disposing of it altogether. Your IT people can do this easily and inexpensively.

IDENTITY THEFT   This threat has become endemic for business travelers, in large part because of RFID chips embedded in passports, credit cards, driver's licenses, keyless building entrance systems and automobiles, to name a few. Using an RFID swiper, all a thief needs to do is move within a few feet of the chip to capture its data. For that reason, it's wise to carry such forms of identification in an anti-static or cloaking bag, which is designed to shield them from RFID detection.

You can't request a passport without an RFID chip anymore, but it's still possible to obtain a driver's license and credit card without one embedded in it. Either way, you should buy a stainless-steel, RFID-shielding wallet case to carry your identification.

Some tips for circumventing identity theft while traveling:

— Carry only the bare minimum identification; your passport is sufficient.

— If you plan to rent a car or otherwise drive a car, check with the American Automobile Association before you depart to obtain an International Driving Permit.

— Take only one or two credit cards – I prefer one VISA and one AMEX. It will simplify things if stolen or used illegally, and it will help you track your expenses more easily. Use a card that allows you to obtain cash advances from travel offices or recognized banks.

— Avoid using debit cards at ATMs located outside of buildings. Thieves can use myriad ways to appropriate your account information from them. If you use an ATM, pick one inside the lobby of a well-known bank.

— If you need medical assistance, you might have to provide your Social Security number. Carry it with your other valuable personal-identification documents. For security, either black out the last four numbers or do not write them down. The best course is to memorize your number.

BIG DATA   This term has become the rage in business these days, but it's making a splash in security circles as well. Essentially, it refers to conducting a link analysis – tracking your phone calls, the Web sites you visit, your banking transactions, credit-card charges, and so forth – to build a profile of your spending and travel habits. Companies can use big data legitimately to locate their most likely customers. But espionage operatives can employ the practice to hone in on potential assets.

Given this new capacity to interpret your transactions, it's important to begin thinking about how your telecommunications, financial and travel behavior could be tipping off operatives about your business intentions.

insider tale
Sarah Palin's Email

In 2008, vice-presidential candidate Sarah Palin's Yahoo email account was hacked by 20-year-old David Kernell. Subsequently, Governor Palin's emails were posted on the Internet. Kernell obtained access to the account by answering her easy password-recovery questions, such as "What year were you born?" and "Where did you go to high school?"

Convicted of two felony counts, Kernell went to prison for a year and a day. But his success wasn't lost on other hackers, so don't forget this lesson about password protection.

19. Many business travelers will no doubt regard a generic laptop and a barebones cell phone as major inconveniences. Doesn't this tactic actually place you at a competitive disadvantage?

It depends how you define "disadvantage." True, temporarily eschewing the latest apps and software will limit your telecommunications capabilities and restrict your entertainment options. But if that's the price for preventing someone from stealing your BI/IP and consequently harming your company's competitive position – or even your personal reputation – it might be worth paying. There's no easy way to play this. It's now the world we live in.

20. Should you take along a disposable cell phone every time you travel for business?

Yes. Doing so means you've begun thinking like a counterintelligence officer. But be sure it's a new phone and/or a new number each time. Always maintain good OPSEC when conducting your business conversations. Clear all contact numbers. Instead, memorize personal and confidential business numbers or cryptically write them down somewhere counterintuitive. Also, always try to buy the least expensive cell phone for your trip, because the cheap ones usually don't have the capability to store spyware.

21. Is it true that the 9/11 terrorists used the Save Draft feature in their email server to communicate with one another; thus they never actually had to transmit the messages? Couldn't I use this same technique to communicate secure messages to my organization?

It is well documented that the 9/11 terrorists shared one email account and used a continuous, unsent draft email to communicate. In the years since that tragic day, however, most law enforcement agencies, intelligence services and computer hackers have grown wise to the trick. Now, if you try this method, you could actually draw attention to yourself.

22. Regarding portable memory sticks that plug into a USB port, would they allow you, essentially, to leave your laptop safely in your room while you carry its brains in your pocket?
Sure, it's a great option to prevent you from having to lug your laptop around every time you go out. Keep in mind, however, that you still need to secure your laptop in your hotel room, because it's vulnerable to an operative entering your room and installing malware or keystroke-capturing software. Be sure to have your IT people inspect it for viruses and wipe it clean each time you return from a trip.

23. What about an IronKey USB flash drive? Does it keep files safe?
IronKey is the brand name of a secure USB flash drive, and it is indeed secure. Its development was funded in part by the U.S. government so individuals transporting sensitive materials could use it for travel. In addition to encrypted protection, the device usually comes with a self-destruct feature: If you enter an incorrect password too many times, the device shuts down permanently. It's expensive, but all savvy businesspeople should travel with one.

Need to know more?
Email us: questions@among-enemies.com

6. Whose Side Are You On?

"And ye shall know the truth, and the truth shall make you free."
— John 8:32, the creed of the Central Intelligence Agency

When They Try to Recruit You

Within the intelligence community, there's an ethos: "Flattery is often the most assured way to garner business intelligence." Consider the following story, factual in every detail.

On a beautiful morning in a great American city, an executive vice president of R&D with a prominent technology company receives an email from the chairman of the computer-science department at a small Italian university. The chairman conveys that he recently read with interest an article the executive had written for a popular trade magazine, and he asks if the executive would be interested in delivering a speech. The university is co-hosting a technology symposium with the European High Technology Foundation to be held in Monaco. Because of the company's leadership in technology development, the symposium would be honored to have the executive give the keynote address. He is flattered to learn they will fly him first class and put him up in a five-star hotel, all for giving a one-hour lecture on his favorite subject. A formal invitation is on its way.

Hours later, a courier delivers an envelope with a handsome invitation printed in gold leaf, along with the airline ticket and hotel reservation. It all seems so straightforward that our executive doesn't think to verify the source. The company's president and PR director are excited for him and anticipate new business opportunities in Europe.

The executive arrives in Nice, and a chauffeured limousine drives him to Monte Carlo, where he's been booked at a fabulous, French Riviera casino-hotel filled with beautiful people. That night, he plays Chemin de Fer and wins a modest amount, attracting the interest of a stunning, raven-haired beauty who tells him, over drinks, that she is of mixed Spanish-Italian ancestry. He is sorely tempted to extend their evening, but he is married, so he wisely resists making further advances and bids her goodnight.

The conference begins the next evening in the hotel ballroom, and after dinner he delivers his prepared remarks to the forty-odd academic and business attendees. During the Q&A session, they ask him many questions, and he grows more and more casual about what he shares. At the closing convocation, he's asked by the department chair if he would be willing to do some consulting for the science foundation and perhaps some lecturing for the university. The chairman intimates that an honorary degree might be offered along with a nominal consulting fee he hopes will not be considered an insult. Flattered beyond belief, our executive is soon sitting in their hip pocket.

Over the next three months, the foundation proposes many junkets, which are always postponed or rescheduled. Meanwhile, the executive is emailing relatively open-source information, along with some of his opinions and ideas, about his company's latest developments. The foundation deposits the consulting fees in a Swiss bank account in his name.

A few months later, an unknown start-up out of Asia introduces a low-cost version of the system the executive's company had been developing for years but had not yet brought to market. The Asian system bears the hallmarks of his ideas for improvement, which his company had seen fit to omit due to cost or complexity.

The effect is staggering. The loss of this potential market nearly puts the company on the ropes. The CEO is outraged and demands a thorough audit of the entire organization to determine if there was a leak. The R&D executive smells a rat and writes his colleague at the university. His email bounces back with a "no such domain" message. He tries to phone the department chair, but the number has been disconnected. He checks his Swiss bank account; it has been closed.

Finally, it hits him. He has been played like a violin in an espionage sonata. Humbled, he goes to the CEO and discloses everything, pleading for understanding as tears run down his face.

Our hapless executive was a victim of a subtle form of recruitment, one of the most effective ways to obtain BI/IP. It occurs when an asset willingly but inadvertently provides secrets or proprietary intelligence to a case officer or handler. The espionage operative, whether government agent or corporate employee – and it could be someone working for both entities – generally uses bribery or blackmail. Sometimes, however, it isn't necessary. As in the above scenario, he or she can fool or flatter a gullible mark into cooperating.

More often, the espionage organization will plant an operative inside a company, seeking an employee who will willingly offer information in exchange for money. This chapter will help you identify situations in which you might be compromised. It will help you avoid falling under the influence of an operative who employs bribery or blackmail in exchange for your cooperation.

insider tale
The Spies Who Weren't

In early January 2011, the news media reported that three high-ranking officials at Renault, the French automaker, were suspected of selling information about the company's new electric-vehicle program. The company paid an unnamed informant US$250,000 for exposing the leak and revealing the three names. After a short investigation, the officials were suspended. A subsequent investigation failed to turn up hard evidence. Rumors spread that China had somehow compromised the men. Then the informant demanded almost US$1 million to reveal written proof.

No evidence of espionage was ever found, but the executives were fired. In March 2011, still with nothing proven, Renault apologized to the three and promised them palliative compensation. The COO, Patrick Pelata, resigned. To this day nothing is certain, although some suspect the company's head of security promulgated the hoax. [18]

In July 2011, Renault debuted its DeZir electric concept car, a joint project with Japan's Nissan auto company, at the Paris Motor Show. It was an enormous hit.

The point of the story is that the threat of espionage became such a major concern to Renault that the company was willing to remove top executives – despite uncertainty about their involvement in espionage – in order to protect its BI/IP.

You came, I was alone,
I should have known,
You were temptation.

So goes the refrain of the old song. Indeed, temptation is possibly the greatest risk the male – and in some instances female – business traveler faces, especially when visiting a foreign country. Somehow, the thought creeps into the brain that the social rules are different abroad, that every pretty girl walking down the sidewalk wants a tryst, that it's okay to eat and drink too much or indulge in other forbidden, inappropriate, dangerous – and often illegal – activities in various dens of iniquity.

The problem is, espionage operatives know how the human brain and other parts of the anatomy operate, and they watch for business travelers exhibiting weakness and look for and plan ways to exploit it.

The two greatest threats to a male business traveler's safety and the preservation of BI/IP assets are alcohol and women. As I've now stated repeatedly, the rule of thumb when traveling is simple: Don't do anything you would not want not to see on the front page of your hometown newspaper.

Sometimes, you don't even have to *do* anything; suggestive photos of you talking and drinking with a woman in a bar can create an opportunity for blackmail and recruitment. At that point, protestations are feeble and likely to fall on deaf ears. After all, everyone knows that boys will play when they're away.

So, don't do it. Don't do anything you wouldn't do when you're home or anything that you wouldn't want your spouse, your children or your colleagues – or superiors – to see on a YouTube video or, worse, on the evening news.

That's what could have happened to Matt, our next protagonist.

Matt has been hired as vice president of finance for a large, multinational, agricultural-chemicals company. Only 29 years old, he sports a resume that includes an MBA from Wharton, a two-year stint as a senator's aide and practical experience working as an investment banker on Wall Street. It doesn't hurt his image that he has his father's famous last name and a hefty trust fund. Life is good:

Matt is newly married to a beautiful woman, twins are on the way, and he's pulling down a basic salary of US$250K.

Matt is on his way to Bangkok, Thailand, to review a potential merger opportunity. At the hotel, the bellboy drops a not-too-subtle hint that he could provide a "masseuse" for a reasonable fee. Matt can't think of a single reason to say no.

Soon thereafter, someone knocks on his door. Matt is surprised to see not one, not two, but three very attractive young Thai girls dressed in shorts and halter tops standing before him.

"You buy two, get one free," the leader explains, as the other two girls giggle.

Powerfully excited by the prospect, Matt welcomes the trio, and a six-handed massage begins. As might be expected, one thing leads to another. Just as money changes hands, however, the room door flies open, and the hotel security director enters, accompanied by two uniformed guards. Frozen in place, wearing nothing but boxer shorts, Matt is taken into custody by the guards, who handcuff him while the girls flee.

For Matt, the room starts to spin. Terrified, he begins to urinate down his leg. The security director sits him down and orders the two guards to leave.

A moment later, another man wearing a dark suit enters and stands in front of Matt. In a disappointed yet authoritative voice, he says, "You are in a lot of trouble, my young friend. You have just been caught in the act of having sex with minors in a country that has zero tolerance for such a thing. The penalty is life in prison."

Matt suddenly feels sick to his stomach.

"There is, however, a way to hide this shame and humiliation from your family, friends and co-workers, and most importantly, to keep you out of prison for the next 50 years. My name is Mr. Chai. I have business interests in this city. I can vouch for you and keep you out of jail, as long as you agree to provide me with certain information about your business dealings from time to time. If you do so, I can make this embarrassing situation go away. Will you help me, or should I ask the officers to return? You must answer now."

A stunned Matt vigorously shakes his head in agreement.

"Good," says Mr. Chai. "I will contact you soon."

Heading toward the door, he stops and turns.

"If you think you can just go back to your country and forget about our agreement or plan to quit your job and start a fresh career, think again. All of your exploits have been recorded. One click of my email Send icon and everyone you have ever known will see your massage session.

"One more thing," he says, smirking. "I hear you are expecting twins. Congratulations."

Mr. Chai exits, and Matt vomits down his bare midriff.

The Recruitment Cycle

Manipulation and instilling fear, the tactics used by Mr. Chai in Matt's case, actually have yielded a poor record of success, to the extent that any intelligence officer knows you can always catch more flies with honey than vinegar. That said, when you're dealing with foreign intelligence agencies and/or private-sector espionage operatives, you can never be certain which methods they'll employ. Just because the CIA will not blackmail doesn't mean your competitor won't.

However it's attempted, the goal is to recruit you. It's a time-tested methodology, known as Human Intelligence or HUMINT, utilized by professional spies around the world. They develop and control, or run, a person known as an asset – a target who has been persuaded by bribery, blackmail, ideology and/or an appeal to the ego to divulge sensitive information.

For example, recruitment is part of the standard curriculum taught to case officers undergoing training at "The Farm," the CIA's not-so-secret facility where young spies learn the practice known as tradecraft. Whether it is conducted by a government intelligence service or the private sector, recruitment functions the same way.

An individual is identified by operatives as a person of interest, someone who might have access to valuable information. The individual, now considered a potential asset, must be courted or coerced then persuaded that giving up intelligence is in their best interests. Therefore, finding the asset's weaknesses and knowing how to

exploit them is critical to recruitment success. That is why operatives of all stripes tend to watch potential assets so closely. Turning
someone into an asset is difficult. As one former CIA instructor at
The Farm liked to say, "You are essentially convincing someone to
make the worst decision of their life."

The recruitment cycle involves a six-step procedure. To persuade
someone to betray their employer or their country, espionage professionals proceed in the following manner:

— Spotting
— Assessing
— Evaluating
— Recruiting
— Handling and, if necessary,
— Terminating

Recruitment is a building-block process. Regardless of whether it involves espionage or national security, those six steps must
be conducted in order. Skipping a step could mean overlooking or
losing essential information and certain confirmations that warrant
taking the next step. An intelligence officer or espionage operative
cannot recruit an asset before that asset has been properly and thoroughly assessed. Most business recruitment is conducted by corporate operatives and rarely by freelance private collectors. From here
on, I will limit the description to those individuals.

Spotting

Spotting an asset is a never-ending process. Operatives are constantly on the lookout for a target that can provide them with access to
intelligence. Where do they seek suitable candidates? Simple; anywhere and everywhere, but here are a few of their more common
haunts:

— Airport lounges
— Hotel lobby bars
— Trade-show floors
— Conferences and business seminars
— Social networking sites (Facebook, LinkedIn and Twitter,
among others)

— Company Web sites

— Political rallies and fundraisers

— Gyms and health clubs

— Private clubs

— Sports leagues or clubs

— Golf courses

— Universities

— Restaurants and bars

— Parties

Spotting an asset is a cultivated skill in observation, much the same as sports scouts develop a keen eye for talented baseball or football players. In your case, are you making their job easier or more difficult?

For example, do you like to party?

Are you careless where you leave your mobile phone or briefcase?

Do you talk a lot about your business and travel, particularly to strangers?

Are you a skirt-chaser?

If so, you will attract spotting. If you show promise, an operative will begin digging into your background, first looking for publicly available information found in Google searches, Web sites and the social media. He or she will then focus more sharply by staking you out – yes, physically observing you. If the surveillance suggests you could be an asset, the operative begins the recruitment cycle in earnest. If he or she finds that you have access to desirable proprietary resources – whether BI/IP, people, software, equipment or anything that works to the advantage of the competition – the operative will target you for the next phase: assessment.

insider tale
Spotting a HUMINT Target
What does the perfect target look like? It all depends on the competitor's operational requirements. If a foreign intelligence service working on behalf of the business interests of the country is looking to recruit someone, say, in the United States to provide sensitive information on a new technology being developed in

Silicon Valley, the target, according to a former CIA case officer, might look something like this:

> The perfect recruitment asset within the U.S. technology sector is a foreign-born male engineer working on a business visa. Chances are he thinks he is much smarter than his American colleagues. Yet, he is disgruntled because he is unappreciated, mistreated or ostracized. He is most likely young to middle-aged; he rents rather than owns, has few friends, is critical of the Western lifestyle – despite behaving hypocritically at times – and has no patriotic ties to the United States or perhaps even to his home country. He would most likely commit espionage out of spite and for personal gain – preferably a large sum of cash.

Assessing

An assessment often begins with the operative striking up a conversation with you, the potential asset. It is not a formal interview; rather, it seems like a friendly chat, and most likely you won't realize you're being assessed for espionage.

Assessing doesn't necessarily begin with a face-to-face interaction, however. The use of email or social media has made both spotting and assessing potential targets much easier. Nevertheless, there is no substitute for human interaction.

Consider this scenario.

Ned is sitting on a bench in the park, next to a drinking fountain, after a 10k run. A man approaches, dressed like Ned in running clothes. He takes a gulp of water and collapses on the bench beside him, breathing heavily.

"Whew!" he says, "It's hot! How long did you run?"

The operative wants to build rapport, and when it is established, he or she will utilize the technique of elicitation as described on page 40.

Elicitation is the subtle means of extracting information during an apparently normal and innocent conversation. Elicitation helps determine whether or not the target has access to useful intelligence as well as a glimpse into his or her personal motivations. Or, put another way, it helps determine whether an individual can be compromised.

Elicitation exploits several fundamental aspects of human nature. Most of us want to be polite and helpful, so we usually respond to questions honestly, even when posed by complete strangers.

In addition, we want to appear well-informed about and proud of our professional specialty, so we might be tempted to say more than we should. We want to be understood and appreciated, so we often feel the need to tell others when we are doing something important and useful. We are similarly predisposed to complain or gripe about our job or our company. Finally, as open and honest people, we are often reluctant to withhold information, lie or be suspicious of another person's motives.

Well-trained espionage operatives can effectively utilize elicitation as a probing technique by playing to these human traits. They can expertly persuade you, the target, to drop your guard and unwittingly divulge information you should not, all the while leaving you thinking, "Wow, what a nice guy (or gal)!"

Here are some telltale signs you're being elicited and assessed for suspect reasons. Watch out for these tactics.

The operative…

— Flatters you into revealing things that should make you suspicious about why a complete stranger would take so much interest in you, your family and your work.

— Agrees with everything you say to a fault, always complimenting or sympathizing with you or telling you how interesting or intelligent you are.

— Engages in active listening and sustained eye contact that makes you feel as though you are the only person in the room, that what you are saying is of the utmost importance.

— Avoids answering questions or talking about himself or herself.

— Repeats and summarizes what you've said as if studying or learning from you, rather than engaging in a simple, casual, back-and-forth conversation.

— Puts you on the defensive from time to time, compelling you to prove you are well-informed.

— Poses leading questions or summations, or intentionally

misunderstands a topic in which you are more knowledgeable or expert, in an attempt to elicit proprietary intelligence.

— Takes the time to respond thoughtfully after you have spoken.

— Offers to pay for the drinks, performs a small favor, or even promises to send you a gift.

— Asks for another get-together.

This isn't to say that everyone with exceptional interpersonal skills is trying to elicit BI/IP from you, but it's important to remember that regardless of someone else's motives, it doesn't make a lot of sense to confide in a complete stranger.

Espionage operatives are trained in assessment. You, performing counter-espionage, need to assess, too. You don't need to share any information with a stranger just for the sake of having a polite conversation.

Ask yourself: *Am I being elicited? What is this person's need to know?*

Whatever questioning techniques the operative employs, suppress your natural instinct to be flattered into responding. Instead of answering questions or setting the facts straight, simply give vague or partial answers, or change the subject.

Better still, begin asking questions of your own. Employ the time-tested techniques of Dale Carnegie. In a polite way, don't be afraid to press the individual to reveal some personal information. If he or she becomes reluctant or uncomfortable, it's a sign you're being elicited.

Last, don't be afraid to be blunt and say you don't wish to discuss the subject, or even that you're not permitted to talk about it without permission from your supervisor or the corporate-communications people. That direct response alone should disqualify you for recruitment – which, of course, would be a good thing.

Evaluating

Do you think you're susceptible to an offer to conduct espionage for the other side? Operatives don't just wander around international trade shows or lurk in coffee shops indiscriminately pitching recruitment to anyone they meet. If they did, they'd probably be arrested quickly or, in some parts of the world, shot dead. Bear in mind that espionage is a crime in many countries, subject to stiff fines and prison sentences.

No. Once the operative has assessed you, both from afar and during elicitation, and suspects you have access to intelligence – as discussed in Chapter 1, the most common target industries are pharmaceuticals, high technology, classified defense projects, financial services and nearly anything having to do with science and engineering – the next step is to build a durable relationship. This is a period of time when the operative evaluates you carefully to determine whether or not you would be amenable to recruitment and willing to provide the BI/IP the competitor seeks. This is perhaps recruitment's most delicate stage.

Catching MICE

Your personal and professional circumstances and motivations are key factors. Indicators that help determine the likelihood you'll play ball are mapped against four widely used criteria – money, ideology, coercion and ego – known within the intelligence community as MICE.

MONEY   What is your financial situation? Do you have debts from gambling or other disreputable activities? Trying to send your kids to expensive private schools you can't afford? Going through a costly divorce?

IDEOLOGY   Do you follow an ideological belief that would allow or compel you to give up BI/IP? Perhaps you feel a moral obligation to level the playing field, or you believe in a global economy, or you're opposed to what you regard as your country's hegemony.

COERCION   Can you be blackmailed into surrendering company secrets? A typical blackmail scenario is being caught on video sleeping with another woman – or, in Matt's unfortunate case, three underage women. If caught, you might agree to cooperate to avoid having your wife or your employer learn of your infidelity. Know this, however: Once you accept money for providing BI/IP, your handlers can continue blackmailing you indefinitely.

EGO   Are you ego-driven; someone who loves the idea of getting back at the company, government or other superiors for, say, being passed over for promotion or failure to recognize your contribution? Or is it simply that you relish the idea of playing the spy?

The four MICE components are perceived weaknesses, each of

which plays a role in turning you into an asset for the competitor's ends. In the aggregate, these weaknesses often determine if you would be most susceptible to bribery or blackmail. Operatives will evaluate all your attributes, positive or negative, and through time-tested assessment methods they'll determine if, and then how, you should be recruited. If so, how can your weaknesses be exploited to turn you into an asset?

insider tale
Birds of a Feather

In 1990, following the devastating losses of U.S. intelligence assets to the Russians at the hands of CIA turncoat Aldrich Ames, then-CIA Director William Webster commissioned a study in an attempt to determine if convicted U.S. spies shared any visible traits. The study, titled Project Slammer, disclosed the following distinctive profile of individuals who committed treason against the United States. Most, if not all, of these traits could apply to a corporate asset as well.

1. All are possessed of a basic belief system that they are…

— Special, even unique

— Deserving of more money, power, recognition, etc.

— In a current situation that is not satisfactory

— Convinced there is no easier option than to engage in espionage

— Only doing what others frequently do

— Not a bad person

— Able to separate performance in their government job, if presently employed, from espionage activities

— Thinks security procedures do not (really) apply to them

2. All are isolated from their espionage actions, because they…

— See their situation in a context in which they face continually narrowing options until espionage seems a reasonable alternative

— See espionage as a victimless crime

— Find it easy to circumvent security safeguards

— Have discovered that ease of accomplishment further reinforces their resolve to continue

3. Their coping behavior regarding espionage activity includes…

— Becoming eager in the initial contact with the hostile intelligence service, including, among some subjects, also feeling thrills and excitement

— After a relationship with espionage activity and a hostile intelligence service has developed, feeling that the process becomes much more bearable, at which point the espionage continues or even flourishes

— In the course of long-term activity, a reconsideration of involvement, to the extent that the glamour subsides and the subject sometimes considers telling authorities what he has done

Recruiting

In business, there is the point called the pitch. It's when the salesman hopes to close the deal. Likewise, in espionage, the closing is known as the pitch. Several months or even years might elapse before a potential asset is considered ripe to pitch. If operatives pitch too soon, or before the individual has been thoroughly vetted, it could frighten that person away or even result in negative repercussions such as exposure or arrest.

Obviously, the operative making the pitch will probably not just come out and say, "Will you spy against your company if I give you money?" Nor will the operative overtly threaten blackmail. Instead, he will lay the incriminating photos on the table then discuss working together for both parties' best interests. In fact, a good espionage operative will spin the pitch quite subtly, using qualifying questions, for example:

"How would you like to do the right thing in your life?"

"Don't you owe it to your family to secure their financial future?"

"You know your company/government is morally corrupt. Why not do something to change all that and be a hero?"

"You have such a beautiful family. Wouldn't it be shame to let this break it apart?"

"You're in trouble and you know it. What if I had a way to make these problems go away?"

If you're the target, you might not know you're being cultivated until you hear the pitch. How would you react if an operative who has been a friend or colleague for some time suddenly asked you to commit espionage against your employer? Although every situation is different, the best response is to tell the person you recognize the pitch as espionage and – this is important –immediately refuse the offer and firmly tell the individual never to speak of it again.

An effective exchange might sound something like this:

Operative: We've been friends a long time. You trust me, right?

Target: Of course I do.

Operative: You have such an amazing family, and I know that as a great husband and father you would do anything to ensure their well-being.

Target: Yes, you know I would. What are you getting at?

Operative: What I'm saying is we've talked in great detail about how your company has been destroying the little guy, acting im-morally on every level and in the long run will put thousands of hardworking people out of a job. We both know it's wrong and that's not the lesson we would teach our kids. Right?

Target: Sure.

Operative: I know a way that you can do the right thing and be well compensated for it; a way to ensure your actions are morally justified and, in the process, provide for your family like never be-fore. I would like you to work for me and my employers.

Target: Quit my job?

Operative: No, absolutely not. We simply want you to provide us with some of your company's documents from time to time. That's it. Your compensation will be $10,000 a month, plus the knowledge that you are making a positive difference.

Target: What? Are you out of your mind?

Operative: Wait. Hear me out. It's not what you think. All I'm saying…

Target: No, *you* wait! Do you think I'm a fool? You're asking me to spy on my company. That's espionage, and it's against the law. I could go to jail for this if I did it, which I won't. Do you think I'm going to jeopardize my career and my family's future? I can't believe what you're suggesting. I've worked here for 15 years. Spy on my own company and hand over all our trade secrets to you? No way!

Operative: No, you totally misunderstood me. This is just a little consulting gig. I…

Target: Bullshit! I understand exactly what you're suggesting. I thought I knew you, but obviously you're not someone I care to know.

Operative: Look, all I'm saying is…

Target: Stop! Don't say another word!

Operative: Come on, now. You're taking this all wrong. I'm your friend. I would never do anything to harm you or your family's future.

Target: No, you're not my friend. Not another word! This conversation is over!

Bear in mind that this moment of recruitment has been in the works for a long time. Espionage operatives are often former intelligence officers. They're master salesmen. Although the target in our scenario was able to dismiss this pitch effectively, the operative was likely prepared with several, more persuasive arguments. Therefore, engaging in debate is risky. End the conversation immediately. The operative will try to spin the situation, as did this one, but don't engage – and immediately report the contact to your company security officer or to human resources.

Handling

If for some misguided reason a target lets himself or herself be recruited to perform espionage, the next stage is handling. As the word implies, the new asset will be assigned to a handler – or, in intelligence parlance, a case officer – who will provide guidance and instructions. Most often, the asset's primary task is obtaining and delivering BI/IP such as internal memos, R&D information, financial or legal documents, company strategy or personnel records.

In 1996, the U.S. Congress passed the Economic Espionage Act. But it wasn't put to use until aerospace engineer Dongfan "Greg" Chung was brought to trial in 2010. Chung had worked in the industry for 30 years, first at Rockwell International and then Boeing, during which time he amassed over 225,000 proprietary documents, which he provided the Chinese government to develop space-shuttle and rocket technologies. Although he claimed to be using the documents to write a book, the evidence indicated he employed multiple ways of smuggling the documents to China. The FBI estimated the value of the stolen intelligence at $2 billion.

Evidence included a letter signed by Chung, stating he wished to aid the "motherland" and contribute to its Four Modernizations program. "Your honor," he said to U.S. District Judge Cormac J. Carney, "I beg your pardon and let me live with my family peacefully." Carney thought otherwise and sentenced the 73-year-old Chung, who was alleged to have amassed a $3 million fortune at the time of his trial, to 16 years in prison.

Chung's misdeeds were discovered during a federal investigation of another Chinese-born, naturalized citizen, Chi Mak, who was tried and found guilty of trying to export military technology. In 2008, Mak was sentenced to 24 years and five months in federal prison.

Terminating

In Robert Ludlum's novel *The Bourne Identity,* and later the movie of the same name, the CIA attempts to terminate a secret operative who lives on to become Jason Bourne. Thanks to Hollywood, most lay people now equate the word with "kill," but in intelligence-speak, terminating an asset simply means to fire him or her – at least in 99 percent of cases.

An asset is commonly terminated because he or she…

— No longer enjoys access to useful intelligence (the most common reason)

— Wishes to quit and/or is becoming uncooperative

— Has been discovered committing espionage, at which point the operative will deny any knowledge of the asset

— Is becoming more of a liability due to behavioral problems or other factors, and

— The intelligence has been compromised or might be used to misinform the operative – in which case the asset has become a double agent and is now working at cross purposes with the competitor or the sponsoring agency.

Termination is the final step in the recruitment process. All assets are eventually terminated, although some can be employed for years. Beyond the reasons listed above, there is yet another way termination occurs: The asset is discovered by the employer or the government, for example through an FBI investigation.

Very few assets ever perform like Donfan Chung or Chi Mak, possessing and passing useful BI/IP for decades. Though the competitor, whether a corporation or a country, commonly walks away having gotten its money's worth, for the asset the spoils are rarely worth the risk. Massive bouts of depression and remorse tend to follow termination, often with catastrophic fallout in the asset's personal and professional life.

Don't let this happen to you. Say no to any offer to perform espionage.

The recruitment cycle has been around since the days of Sun Tzu. It will certainly be around for a long time to come. Manipulating assets began in warfare and graduated to governmental diplomacy, but today the practice of stealing intelligence is most prevalent in business. As a business traveler, when you fully understand the threat of espionage and, in particular, the dangers in recruitment, you will greatly reduce your odds of becoming a target.

In other words, you can ensure your security when you think and act like a counterintelligence officer.

insider tale
Loyalty, Like Glory, Can Be Fleeting

Consider this observation from Peter Earnest, a former CIA spokesman who is now executive director of the International Spy Museum in Washington, D.C. This passage is from his book *Business Confidential: Lessons for Corporate Success from Inside the CIA*: "Loyalty to country is a concept that most Americans, and most people of other nationalities, believe and live by. Loyalty to the company that employs you – as opposed to one that you or a relative founded – doesn't necessarily carry the same weight or sense of transcendence." [19]

24. Do operatives avoid business travelers with Ivy League educations? Wouldn't they be wary of exceptionally smart people?

It's just the opposite. Ivy League types are exactly the kind of people operatives are looking for. They play to their egos, reinforcing the idea they're smarter than the others they work with. One approach is to declare that the mark is far too bright to be caught by less-well-educated workmates. They'll also offer more money than the mark is making – no matter what the amount is – portraying it as a fitting reward for someone so gifted.

The government's files are full of such cases.

25. If you realize you're being pitched to spy, should you play along to learn more about the plot against your company?

No! This is a job strictly for a *trained* counterintelligence officer, someone who has been practicing tradecraft for years. The best espionage operatives are extremely clever. They will see right through you. Plus, as part of the handling process, they will test, or vet, you from time to time to assess your loyalty. Never become involved in the espionage process. If you think you are being pitched, end the conversation. Get out quickly, and leave the rest to trained professionals.

26. What if you have signed a consulting retainer confidentially with another firm? If they haven't presented a pitch to spy, is it safe to continue the relationship?

If you've been moonlighting as a consultant, and your present employer doesn't permit it, stop right away. If it is acceptable to consult on the side, inform the company for whom you're consulting – in writing – and likewise state that you fully comply with the Economic Espionage Act of 1996. State that in no way would you ever divulge BI/IP belonging to your current employer.

If you are being evaluated by operatives, they probably will conclude that you are not a good candidate for recruitment and cancel your contract. On the other hand, if they are intelligence professionals, they might accept your agreement to keep you happy and build trust, and still pitch you later down the road. Rely on your instincts.

27. How do you ensure that recruitment is not occurring within your organization?

If you are genuinely concerned, try hosting an espionage-awareness course for your entire staff. Following the course, offer to meet confidentially with individuals who suspect they have been approached by operatives.

28. I suspect that my company has been penetrated by an espionage operative. How can I find out for certain?

First, conduct a vulnerability assessment of your company's IT network. Next, consider performing a full-scope security assessment to determine if there's an insider, competitor or foreign intelligence service threat. At Security Management International LLC, we recommend a process known as the CARVER Target analysis and Vulnerability Assessment Methodology. CARVER is an intelligence/special operations community acronym that stands for criticality, accessibility, recognizability, vulnerability, effect and recuperability. SMI has performed this type of assessment for companies and U.S. military installations to detect espionage penetrations.

Need to know more?
Email us: questions@among-enemies.com

7. Here, There and Everywhere

*"A man who wishes to make a profession of goodness
in everything must necessarily come to grief
among so many who are not good."*
– Niccolò di Bernardo dei Machiavelli, *The Prince*

Where Espionage Threats Are Greatest

As you've discovered in these pages, espionage is all around you. Some countries pose a greater threat than others, but all share certain commonalities.

In Chapter 1, you learned never to assume you're not under surveillance by espionage operatives, and the places where you are most at risk are airports, taxis and hotel rooms.

In Chapter 5, you learned that the portable technologies you use for conducting business are vulnerable to espionage – particularly your laptop and mobile phone. As I've stressed over and over, it's unwise to expose these devices to public Wi-Fi networks or to use them in confined areas such as taxis and hotel rooms, where there is a high likelihood you are being surveilled. And I've warned you never to carry sensitive BI/IP on your hard drive.

You should never be separated from your assets. When it is in your power to do so, give no one – particularly officials of a foreign government, such as customs or immigration personnel – permission to take your computer, phone or USB flash drive away to a room or area in which you are not present. Be aware, however, that per international law, customs and immigration personnel are authorized to detain travelers and inspect their luggage and belongings, at least for short periods of time. Be prepared for this eventuality, and decide in advance how you will deal with it if it happens to you.

This chapter identifies the countries posing the greatest threats to the business traveler, and it is intended to help you prepare yourself for those destinations. I encourage you to confer with your company's security people for more current or detailed information. They should be able to provide training and travel briefings specific to your work or industry.

The Most Eager

In 2005, the U.S. Office of the National Counterintelligence Executive, the NCIX, reported that at least 108 countries were engaged in economic, industrial – and, in some cases, military – espionage. If you travel to Afghanistan, China, Cuba, Egypt, France, India, Iran, Iraq, Israel, Japan, Korea (North and South), Nigeria, Pakistan, Russia, Taiwan, Thailand, the United Arab Emirates and the United Kingdom, you need to take the greatest precautions. These 18 countries are among the most eager to appropriate your BI/IP for their own purposes. Or, they harbor the greatest number of espionage operatives from all over the world. In general terms, here is a brief characterization of each country's dangers and threats.

Afghanistan   Despite the U.S. military drawdown, Afghanistan remains a very dangerous place. Aside from the obvious physical threats of kidnapping, street crime, terrorism and unexploded ordnance, businesspeople looking to invest in Afghanistan need to realize that no secure telecommunications infrastructure has been established. This means every cell phone, email and other form of electronic communication is monitored by numerous third parties at all times. In addition, government enforcement against such acts is non-existent, so there is nothing to deter electronic surveillance and eavesdropping.

China   In 2010, the FBI prosecuted more Chinese espionage cases than at any time in our nation's history, and FBI Director Mueller has commented in many speeches that China is stealing our secrets for developing its military technology and economic capability. [20]

Small wonder. The United States and China now enjoy the most highly developed trade relationship of any two countries in the world, although each holds a very different view of the legal and ethical ways to collaborate in those business dealings. China has been acknowledged by many U.S. government sources as the leader in economic espionage. It began in the 1980s, when former Chinese leader Deng Xiaoping launched the 863 Program. It was designed to put China on a fast track to technological equality with the developed nations of the world by taking advantage of the emerging computer revolution. It emphasized "achieving breakthroughs and shortcuts across a wide spectrum of military and industrial technologies."

Deng's program might seem innocent and logical, but to achieve it he deployed not only the country's external security services but also its internal service, which monitors visitors to China. Moreover, he issued an underground obligation, or order, stating that Chinese citizens traveling abroad and/or having business relationships with foreign partners must share what they learn with the government.

As the program proceeded and intelligence efforts acquired vital technologies – and, in some cases, entire weapons systems – Chinese engineers and scientists quickly adapted them via reverse engineering. The Chinese also exploited the U.S. immigration system, which grants foreigners opportunities equal to those of American citizens. Untold numbers of Chinese have been hired by American companies, often in engineering and scientific positions, and many have operated as spies for their homeland. China also extracts BI/IP from its students attending U.S. colleges and universities. As a result, the United States and China represent the economic-espionage battleground of the present as well as the future.

If you have been traveling or are planning to travel to China, make no mistake: China is the world's biggest offender when it comes to espionage. Business travelers there – and in Hong Kong and Taiwan as well – have a greater chance of being electronically surveilled than not. Take every possible precaution, all of which have been detailed in these pages.

Cuba   Just because Fidel Castro is no longer this tiny island nation's official leader doesn't mean Cuba doesn't still possess impressive intelligence capabilities. Granted, the Soviet Union provided Cuba's financial backing during the Cold War, and its technological capabilities are now rudimentary, but basic human-intelligence techniques, such as elicitation, physical surveillance, blackmail, bribery and recruitment have become well polished over more than six decades. The bottom line: Never underestimate the effectiveness of a Cuban intelligence officer.

Egypt   No question, former President Hosni Mubarak held a tight grip on Egypt, and maintaining such power for decades, especially in a country with extremely high unemployment, cannot be accomplished without strong access to information from a capable intelligence service. Now, the Arab Spring has removed Mubarak from power, and the remaining vacuum has attracted spies from around the globe interested in learning what will happen next. The problem has grown so intense that Cairo television commercials warn Egyptian citizens to be on the lookout for foreign spies, even showing examples of what a spy looks like and how one might act.

France   As mentioned earlier, French intelligence has openly admitted to spying on international business travelers. Most travelers, particularly tourists, would never dream that a trip to Paris could become a dangerous proposition. In reality, however, the French have always been good at surveillance, due in large part to the influx of Arabs who immigrated from North Africa, as well as the economic need to stay abreast of technological advancements to maintain their global status.

India   "An entire gamut of corporate espionage is happening around us, and it is a huge industry by itself," says Pavan Duggal, a cyber law expert and Supreme Court advocate.[21] India has seen a tremendous jump in the size of its middle class over the past decade, due in large part to an educated, hard-working generation of young people proficient in a wide range of technologies. Despite its recent economic success, India remains a relatively poor nation. Seeing how the newly rich are enjoying the good life, more Indians want a slice of the pie, and therefore many are engaging in espionage. According to the Associated Chambers of Commerce and Industry of India, over 35 percent of companies operating in various sectors across the country are performing espionage to gain advantage over their competitors. Some are even spying on their employees via social-networking Web sites.

Iran   Notorious for its religious authoritarianism, its political repression and its relentless drive to become a nuclear power, the Iranian government has been aggressively pursuing espionage, including arresting tourists and business travelers to extort information from them and their employers.[22] As the FBI reports, "One recent case, called Wintry Blast, was opened when our Minneapolis

Field Office uncovered a major Iranian procurement network operating through front companies in Asia. The network was seeking export-controlled U.S. technology for the Iranian military and for Iran's ballistic missile programs." [23]

For those traveling to Iran, particularly from the West, Iranian intelligence likely will place you under surveillance from the moment you cross the border. Even if you are attempting to do business with the government, they often will accuse you of being a foreign spy until you can prove their suspicions unfounded – an unlikely prospect.

Iraq   Much like Afghanistan, Iraq's secure telecommunications network is weak. Add the influx of foreign investors and entrepreneurs looking to capitalize on the country's massive but neglected oil resources, and you open the door to all kinds of espionage. No question, Iraq has become a spy den in the Middle East.

Israel   As the world's only Jewish state, and surrounded by enemies, Israel operates in a mode of perpetual – and justifiable – paranoia. It is highly suspicious of outsiders and plays its geopolitical cards close to its vest. The Mossad, Israel's world-renowned intelligence service, has a reputation that often takes on legendary proportions. For personal security reasons alone, business travelers should expect a lack of privacy when visiting Israel. Act suspiciously in any way and you soon could observe the Mossad's prowess firsthand. As one famous story goes, a CIA officer returned to his hotel room in Tel Aviv, only to see two feet disappearing up through the ceiling tiles.

Japan   As the world's most homogeneous nation, Japan exhibits business peculiarities. The one of most concern is its degree of espionage, which often is the rule and not the exception. In fact, Japan is considered a world leader in private-sector espionage. It earned that distinction via two very public indictments in U.S. courts under the Economic Espionage Act. One involved the theft of research at the Cleveland Clinic Foundation by Japanese scientists. The other concerned patent infringement on Paice LLC, an American microprocessor maker, by Toyota.

Foreign businesspeople working in Japan should assume that their Japanese partners and competitors alike have attempted as much espionage as possible on them, and they won't hesitate to engage in such behavior if it means gaining even the slightest competitive advantage.

Korea   It is obvious that North Korea is a tight-fisted police state where hyper-surveillance and lack of personal freedom are the keys to young Kim Jong-un's survival. As much as North Korea spies on everyone within its borders, however, South Korea has become known as a country where international business travelers should keep close tabs on their R&D secrets.

Nigeria   Almost any country you visit in Africa is bound to be economically disadvantaged. But when visiting Nigeria, business travelers need to be especially vigilant. Known for its vast oil, ridiculous Internet scams – known by the FBI as the Nigerian 419 scams – and Lagos, one of the world's fastest-growing cities, spying in Nigeria is epidemic. Government and corporate corruption often provide competitors with instant access to intelligence. Doing legitimate business in Nigeria is extremely difficult.

Pakistan   Among the nations of the Middle East and Southwest Asia, Pakistan has always been especially steeped in paranoia, borne out of its hatred for its nuclear neighbor, India. Worse, the stealthy killing of Osama bin Laden by U.S. Navy SEALs in 2011 rendered Pakistan even more on edge. Taliban and al-Qaeda fighters move in and out of the country through Afghanistan, and the ISI, the nation's intelligence service, constantly attempts to track everyone even remotely suspicious. All of which makes Pakistan a state where, in terms of physical as well as cyber security, all bets are off.

Russia   The unmasking in 2010 of a network of 10 Russian agents implanted on American soil revealed that these spies had been tasked to collect economic as well as political and military intelligence. The Cold War might be officially over, but according to the FBI there are more Russian intelligence officers operating within the United States than ever before. When Moscow opened its doors to the free-market economy in the 1990s, Westerners were encouraged to do business in the new Russia. At the same time, however, trade shows, tourist attractions and investment opportunities became hot spots for GRU (formerly KGB) officers to apply their intelligence tradecraft – and they don't miss much.

Taiwan   The Republic of Taiwan is a country that has for years sought its own identity apart from China. This independence, although not recognized by the mainland government, has forced Taiwan to strive for strong international alliances. Much like Israel, Taiwanese officials are suspicious of everyone. That should be a warning sign to business travelers to be alert for Taiwan's efforts to strengthen its defenses through espionage.

Thailand   With its tropical climate, somewhat stable government – bloodless coups excluded – liberal visa requirements and high number of transients, Thailand has become a spy playground. Its anything-goes atmosphere encourages travelers to let down their guard, making them vulnerable to blackmail or bribery.

United Arab Emirates   Much like Thailand, the UAE is a playground, particularly Dubai. But espionage is never a kid's game. With mega-million deals often conducted over coffee each morning, you can be sure espionage operatives are lurking about. As the old adage goes, they will be following the money.

United Kingdom   Public surveillance in the capital of the country comprising Great Britain and Northern Ireland is more prevalent than in any other city in the world. The British government conducts it to assure the citizenry of physical security and protection against terrorism, and security performed exceedingly well during the 2012 Olympics. What it often can't do successfully is protect business travelers from espionage. As a world transportation hub, London has an extremely diverse population and is a popular spot for operatives of all stripes.

Where to Find Help

Espionage is a crime most businesspeople would prefer not to discuss. It's just as embarrassing to admit you've been the victim of BI/IP theft as it is to reveal you've been hacked. For that reason, it's difficult to know who has been victimized and where to obtain useful advice or feedback.

In the United States, the government has been stepping up to help out. The following agencies are spearheading the mission to educate businesspeople about espionage and protect them from it.

Federal Bureau of Investigation   The FBI could be the most outspoken and aggressive force in this struggle. The bureau certainly leads in prosecuting espionage operatives under the Economic Espionage Act.

In testimony before a congressional committee, C. Frank Figliuzzi, assistant director of the FBI's Counterintelligence Division, described a media campaign the bureau launched in May 2012.

"The campaign [highlighted] the insider threat relating to economic espionage. [It] included print and television interviews, billboards along busy commuter corridors in nine leading research areas nationwide, and public information on the FBI Web site. Through this campaign, the FBI hopes to reach the public and business communities by explaining how the insider threat affects a company's operations and educating them on how to detect, prevent, and respond to threats to their organizations' proprietary information. Perhaps the most important among these is identifying and taking defensive measures against employees stealing trade secrets." [24]

Central Intelligence Agency   The CIA is keenly aware of economic and industrial espionage and is actively fighting it worldwide. In 2004, the agency helped Congress revise and update the Intelligence Reform and Terrorism Prevention Act. The new law's language states, "To win the war on terrorism, the United States must assign to economic and diplomatic capabilities the same strategic priority that is assigned to military capabilities." In other words, the agency treats espionage on a par with terrorism. [25]

Incidentally, *The CIA World Factbook* can be a valuable online reference to learn up-to-the-minute information about various countries prior to travel.

Office of the National Counterintelligence Executive
In addition to assisting all of the U.S. intelligence services, both domestic and military, NCIX is also a repository of information about intelligence matters. On its Web site you can find reports and other information concerning the most critical counterintelligence issues, as well as news and announcements of counter-espionage training and related events.

National Security Agency/Central Security Service   The geeks and techies work in droves for this amalgam. Its mission is to collect, process and disseminate intelligence from foreign electronic signals or other sources. Much of this effort supports military operations, but it also attempts to prevent foreign adversaries from gaining access to classified information, which has over the past decade or so grown to include economic intelligence.

In a speech given in July 2012, General Keith B. Alexander, the NSA director, discussed the ever-growing threat posed by technology and his agency's efforts to counter it. Alexander stated that over a hundred countries now possess the capability to exploit our online systems, and they do so with alacrity. That's why the NSA/CSS has endeavored to become a trusted source of information and statistics for anyone striving to know more about the technological aspects of espionage.

Overseas Security Advisory Council   OSAC, an agency within the Department of State, is a joint collaboration with the private sector to help ensure the safety and security of business travelers and their assets. Prior to departing on a trip to a foreign country, regardless whether you have been there before, it's always wise to obtain the most accurate and up-to-date information about that country's political and social status – including risks and threats to business travelers.

OSAC issues daily email warnings for specific regions and countries. Topics range from physical security and espionage threats to local street scams and notices about geopolitical unrest. Likewise, OSAC's country reports are especially useful for tracking Internet fraud, which is on the rise everywhere. All international business travelers and corporate security officers should sign up for their free bulletins, and they should have OSAC's Web site bookmarked.

Information, Intelligence and Intuition

We live in a society of information overload, using brains whose processing and synthesizing ability hasn't changed much over many centuries. It's entirely possible to obtain far more information regarding threats to your BI/IP, and the places where you're traveling, than you can manage.

That's where your training in counter-espionage comes into play. Its purpose, as I've strived to explain, is to help you sift through those vast amounts of information, which include not just what you can find on a Web site but also what your five senses and intuition tell you. Your senses are direct receptors for interpreting information and turning it into applied intelligence. By using your intuition, which operates like a sixth sense, you become capable of making quick, accurate assessments of what's occurring around you. You can use those assessments to make decisions regarding your personal safety and that of your valuable BI/IP.

There's no magic to doing this. We're all capable of learning how to perform counter-espionage – to become a counterintelligence officer. All it requires is the desire and some training. Reading this book has set you on the path to achieving that objective.

insider tip
Commercial

Business executives from all walks of life can be trained to operate as counterintelligence officers. For more information on how best to protect your organization's corporate secrets, please contact Security Management International, LLC by phone at 703-962-1545 or via email training@smiconsultancy.com.

28. If espionage is so widespread, why aren't more governments working to prevent it?

Espionage is one of those gray areas, because everybody *is* doing it. But it's only illegal in certain countries, such as the United States, and only if a country or operative gets caught in the act. The U.S. government is actively trying to prevent it on an international level, but if other countries agree to enact U.S. laws, they will essentially be killing their own golden goose.

29. What about other countries with corrupt or repressive governments not included on the list such as Burma, Syria and the "Stan" (Central Asian) countries?

Yes, there are other high-threat countries for espionage. In fact, I could write something about nearly every country in the world when it comes to this topic, and I hope the resources provided in these pages will help you personalize your own travel cheat sheet. But I confined the list to countries visited by U.S. business travelers where they will most likely encounter espionage operatives.

30. You mentioned Cuba, but what about Venezuela, Nicaragua, Bolivia and Brazil in Latin America? Don't they have friendly relations with Cuba? Shouldn't they be destinations of concern as well?

Yes, Latin America, particularly Brazil and Mexico, is a booming region for economic growth and thus espionage. It's also a region of the world where personal safety can be tenuous. You need to be extremely vigilant at all times in Latin American countries.

31. What's the best agency to call or email for information before leaving on an overseas business trip?

Your first point of contact prior to an overseas business trip should be your company's internal security office. They will usually have updated information on the country you visiting, often through

OSAC, which I described in the list of agencies above, or a private organization specializing in security travel information.

32. If you fall under surveillance in another country, should you contact the police?

It depends on the country. In some places, it might be the local police who have been assigned to follow you by the government intelligence service. They might also have been corrupted by outside interests. Your best move if you feel threatened is to contact your embassy or consulate.

33. Can your own embassy or consulate in the country you're visiting provide information or assistance?

If you have fallen victim to espionage while overseas, contact your embassy or consulate's regional security officer or the FBI's legal attaché. How much help they can offer is assessed on a case-by-case basis in accordance with international law. Your best defense is to use what you have learned in this book to help ensure that you never have to find out the answer to that question.

Need to know more?
Email us: questions@among-enemies.com

Afterword

> "The success of any trap lies in its fundamental simplicity."
> – Robert Ludlum, *The Bourne Identity*

I wrote *Among Enemies: Counter-Espionage for the Business Traveler* to address a particularly perplexing problem: a crime that occurs hundreds of times each day but goes mostly unobserved, unacknowledged and unpunished. Yet, it is not a victimless crime, because it causes untold losses of competitive advantage to the businesses that create and support our economy. When U.S. businesses are beaten to market by overseas companies that have stolen their BI/IP, it results in a loss of revenues and jobs.

Bottom line: Espionage damages the bottom line.

In many ways, business represents the new battleground, replacing conventional warfare, because espionage is much cheaper than warfare and offers countries a faster, greater opportunity to achieve nationalistic dominance. Economic warfare – and not friendly competition – defines the relationship between the United States and China, but any country, large or small, also can play. And they do. The threats to our most precious resource, our creativity and innovation, are constantly under siege from the three types of operatives I have described.

As I hope I've made clear here, I believe this is a threat we should take seriously. We intelligence officers have a slang name for undercover operatives: ghosts. The enemies around you are, by and large, phantoms; you probably will never see them or know what they have done. That is why vigilance is so important. Your task in performing counter-espionage is almost entirely defensive. You must protect your valuable intelligence by every means possible while never letting operatives know you are on to them or taking any offensive action.

OPSEC is a tough job. I know, because I have been doing it for a long time. The best part of the job is knowing that, at the end of the day, you've done your very best to protect your company's – and your nation's – most important resources.

By all means, never forget the need for diligence.

Safe travels!

ACKNOWLEDGMENTS

After years of being encouraged to write a book by family and friends, I finally took the plunge. I must say it was a lot more challenging than I imagined. Transferring lecture notes and overseas "war stories" into pages of coherent sentences is far more difficult than it sounds. Therefore, I would like thank the following people for their contribution to this book:

Jack B. Rochester guided me step-by-step through the writing process and provided me with invaluable advice, constructive consultation and hours of editing. What started as an inquiry from a payphone in the Middle East to Jack's home in Massachusetts has evolved into a book I am very proud of. Jack is not only a business colleague but someone whom I now call a friend.

To my publisher, Phil Berardelli, and the good people at Mountain Lake Press, thank you for sharing my vision. Together I hope we will fulfill the promise of enlightenment I am committed to sharing with fellow business travelers.

To my mentors, the late Mick Donahue, who gave me my first break in this crazy line of work, and Jon Monett, who has continued to support and counsel me for so many years, I can never thank you for all you have done. Sincere appreciation to all my coaches along the way who have instilled the toughness in me to be thick-skinned and always believe that nothing is impossible.

Last but not least, heartfelt thanks to my unbelievable family. You have always been there for me through good times and bad.

Notes

1. United States Congress, House Sub-committee on Counter Terrorism and Intelligence, Committee on Homeland Security. "Economic Espionage: A Foreign Intelligence Threat to American Jobs and Homeland Security." 112th Congress, 2nd Session. June 28, 2012.

2. Decker, Brett M., and William C. Triplett. *Bowing to Beijing: How Barack Obama Is Hastening America's Decline and Ushering a Century of Chinese Domination.* Washington, D.C.: Regnery, 2011.

3. Enterprise Security Risk Management: How Great Risks Lead to Great Deeds. The CSO Roundtable of ASIS International, April 2010.

4. Starr, Greg. Remarks before annual Overseas Security Advisory Council (OSAC) conference, November 2011.

5. Alperovitch, Dmitri. *Revealed: Operation Shady RAT.* Santa Clara, California: McAfee, 2011.

6. *Annual Report to Congress on Foreign Economic Collection and Industrial Espionage.* NCIX, 2007.

7. Corera, Gordon. "MI5 Fighting 'astonishing' Level of Cyber-attacks." BBC News, June 25, 2012.

8. Shaw, Gaylord. "Lonetree Guilty on All 13 Counts in Spy Trial : First Marine to Draw Espionage Conviction Could Get Life Term." Los Angeles Times, August 22, 1987.

9. Sun Tzu, and Griffith, Samuel B. The Art of War. London: Oxford University Press, 1971.

10. Nasheri, Hedieh. *Economic Espionage and Industrial Spying.* Cambridge: Cambridge University Press, 2005.

11. Nairn, Geoff. "Your Wall Has Ears." *Wall Street Journal,* October 18, 2011.

12. Perlroth, Nicole. "Traveling Light in a Time of Digital Thievery." *The New York Times.* February 11, 2012.

13. Ostrovsky, Victor, and Hoy, Claire. *By Way of Deception: The Making and Unmaking of a Mossad Officer.* New York: St. Martins, 1990.

14. Dickey, Christopher. "Parlez-Vous Espionage?" *Newsweek*, September 22, 1991.

15. Mueller, Robert S., III. Remarks before RSA Cyber Security Conference, San Francisco, California, March 1, 2012.

16. Dolgow, Michael. "Cyberwars Reach a New Frontier: The Airport." *Business Week*, August 15, 2012.

17. Risen, James and Lichtblau, Eric. "Spy Suspect May Have Told Chinese of Bugs, U.S. Says." *The New York Times,* April 15, 2003.

18. Jolly, David. "Renault's Sensational Case of Stolen Secrets Is Dissolving for Lack of Proof." *The New York Times*, March 11, 2011.

19. Earnest, Peter, and Karinch, Maryann. *Business Confidential: Lessons for Corporate Success from Inside the CIA.* Washington, D.C.: AMACOM, 2010.

20. Gertz, Bill. "FBI Calls Chinese Espionage Substantial." *The Washingtion Times.* July 27, 2007.

21. Phadnis, Shilpa, and Joseph-Tejaswi, Mini. "Corporate Espionage on the Rise in India." *The Economic Times,* September 24, 2010.

22. "Iran Arrests 12 'CIA Spies' for Targeting Nuclear Plans." BBC News. November 24, 2011.

23. Mueller, Robert S., III. Remarks before Annual Update Conference on Export Controls and Policy, Washington, D.C., July 18, 2012.

24. United States Congress, House Subcommittee on Counter Terrorism and Intelligence, Committee on Homeland Security. "Economic Espionage: A Foreign Intelligence Threat to American Jobs and Homeland Security." 112th Congress, 2nd Session. June 28, 2012.

25. *Intelligence Reform and Terrorism Prevention Act,* Public Law 108–458. December 17, 2004.

Index